HALLOWEEN

GRAFFITI

COLORING BOOK

BELONGS to:

....

DARK NIGHT

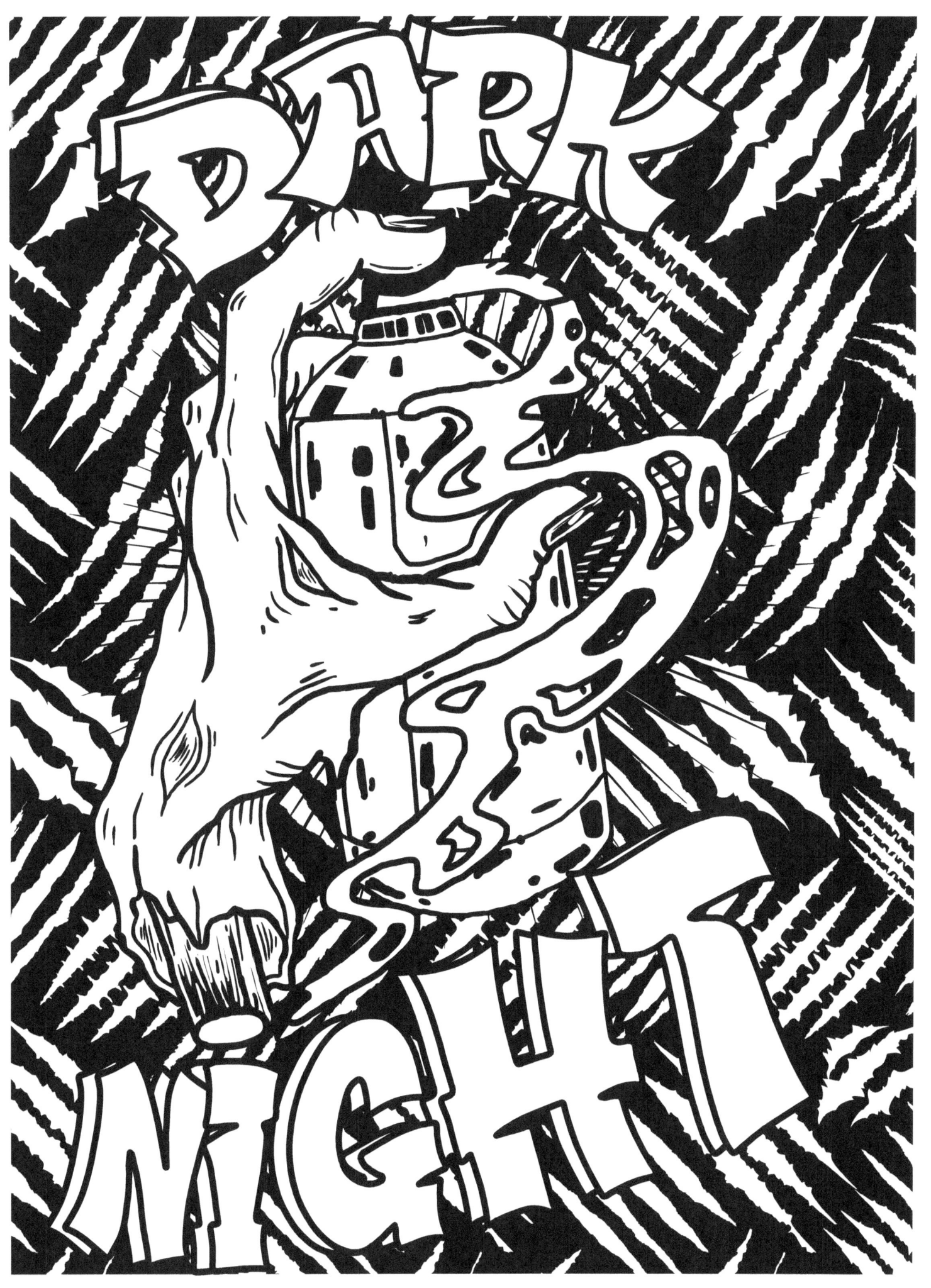

ZOMBIE

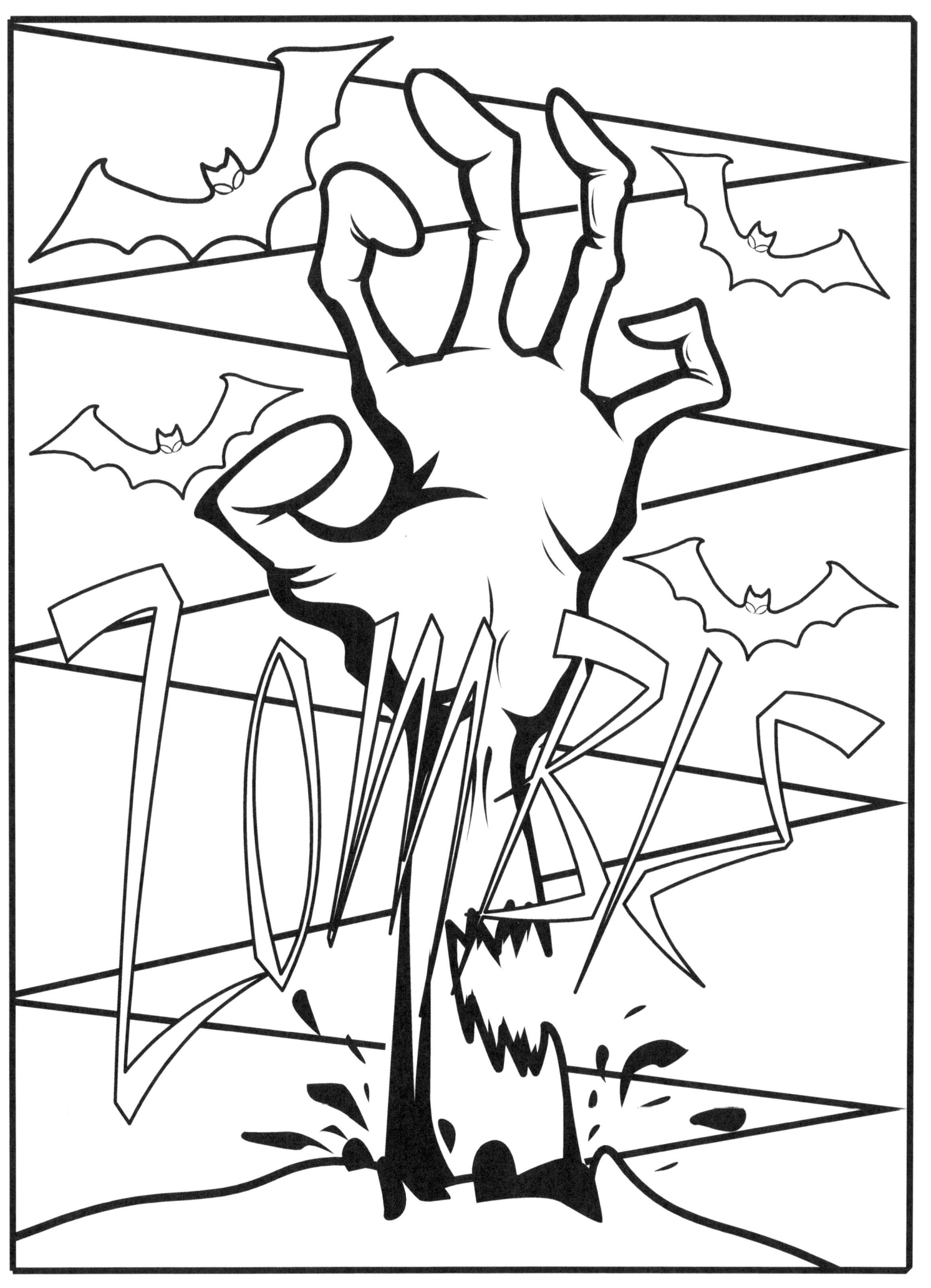

mummy

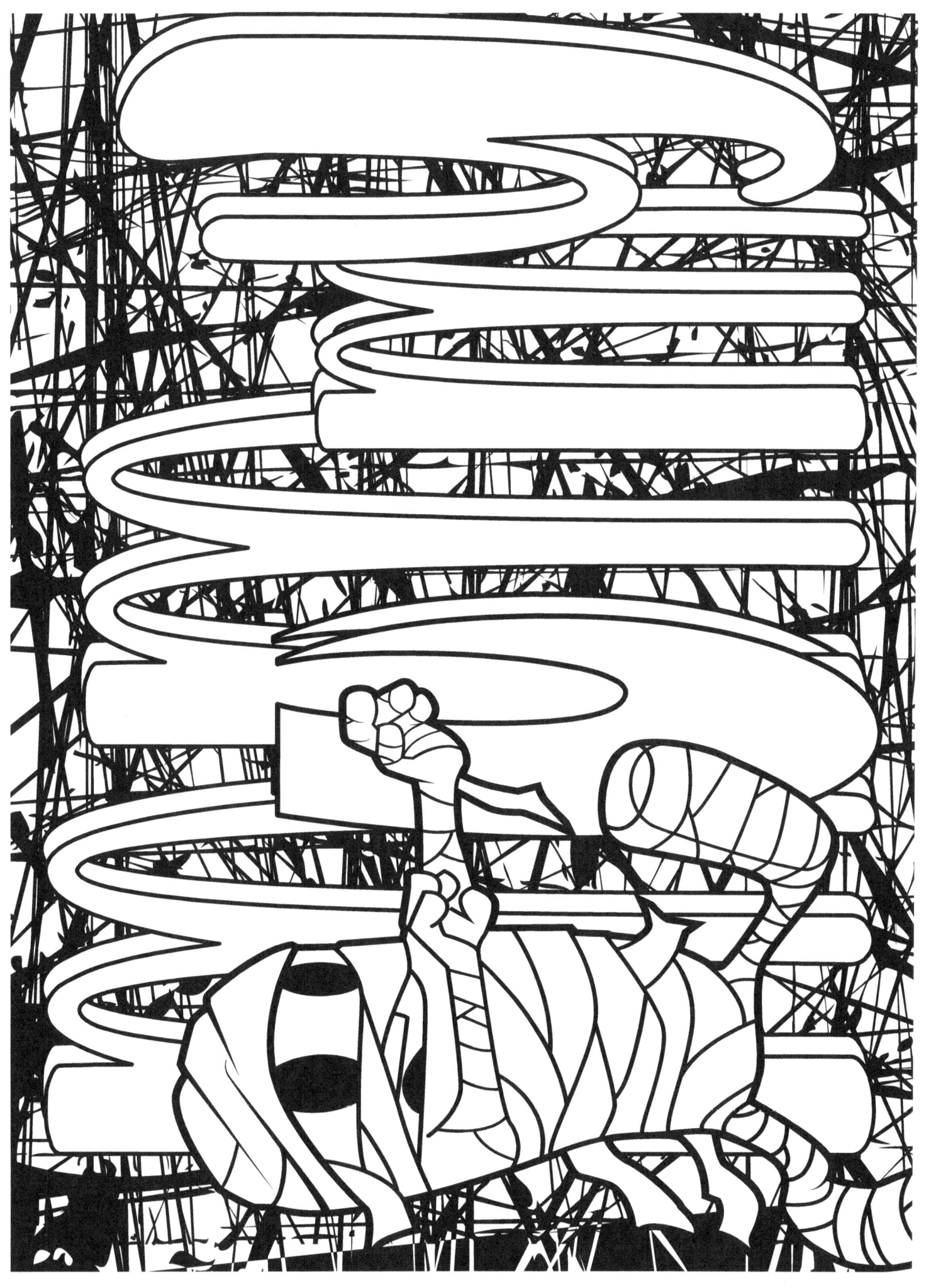

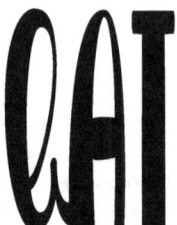

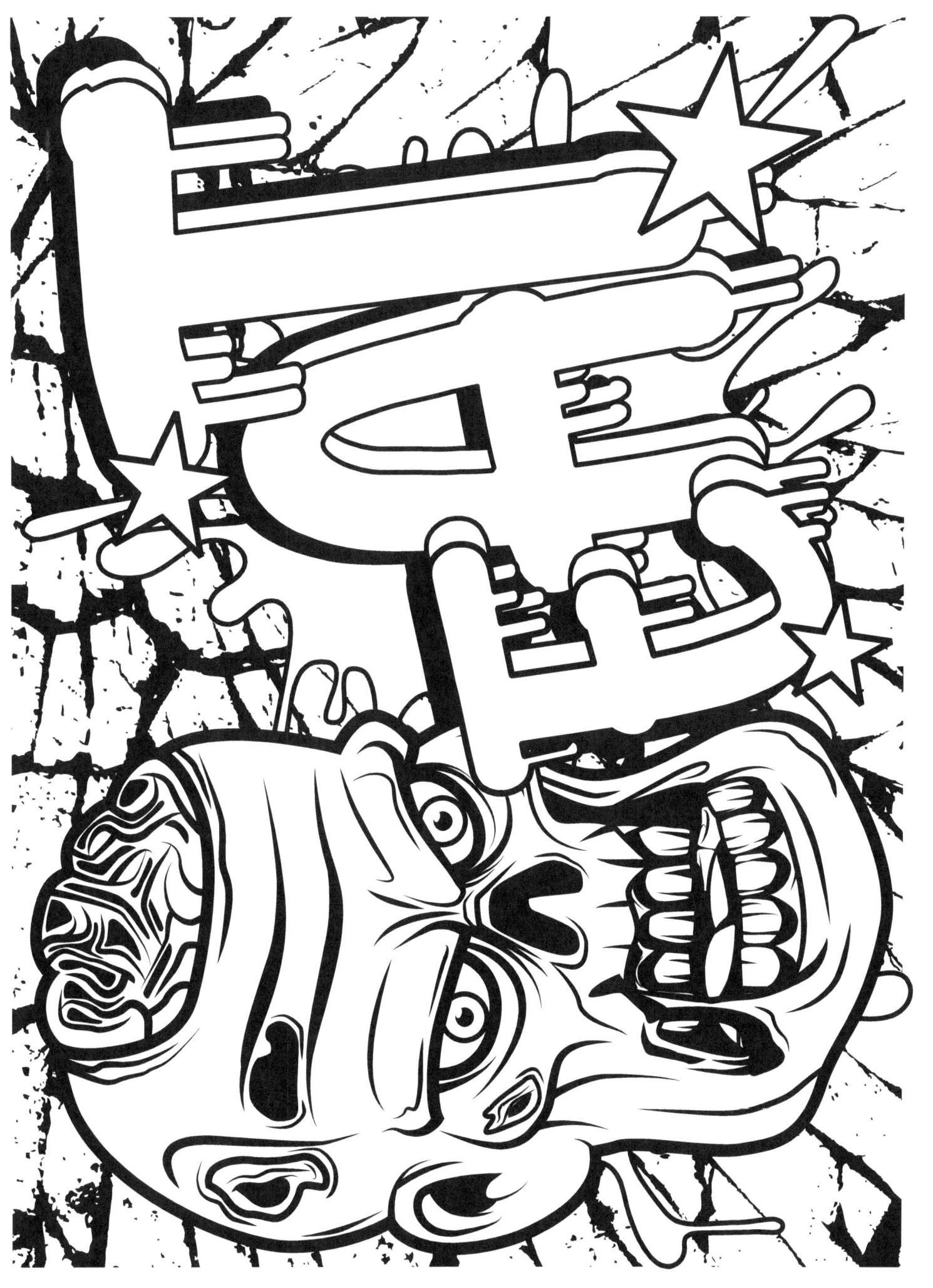

HALLOWEEN

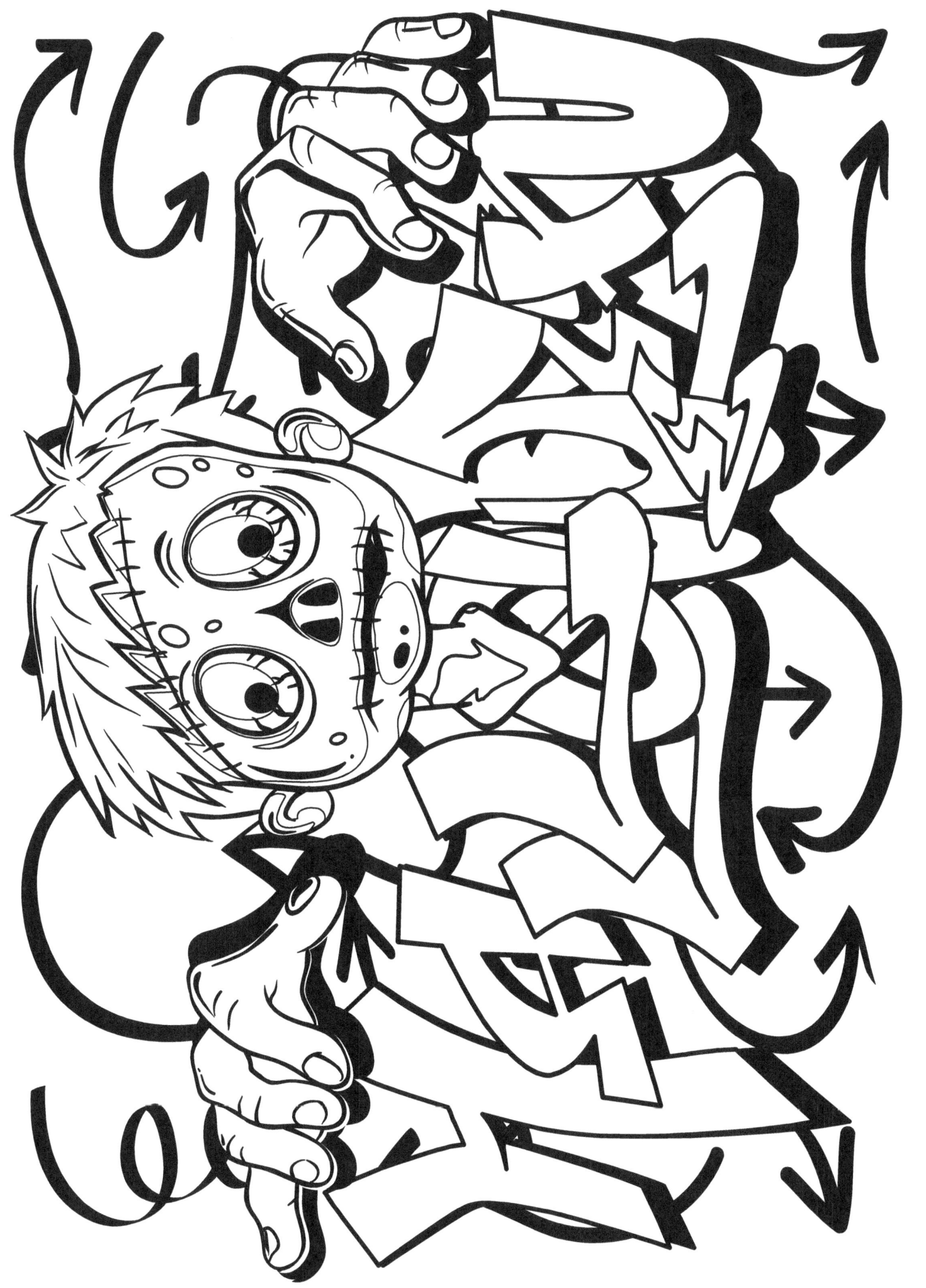

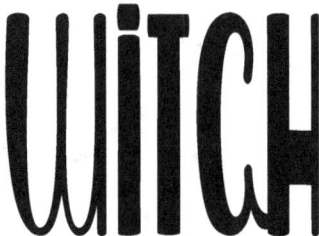
WITCH

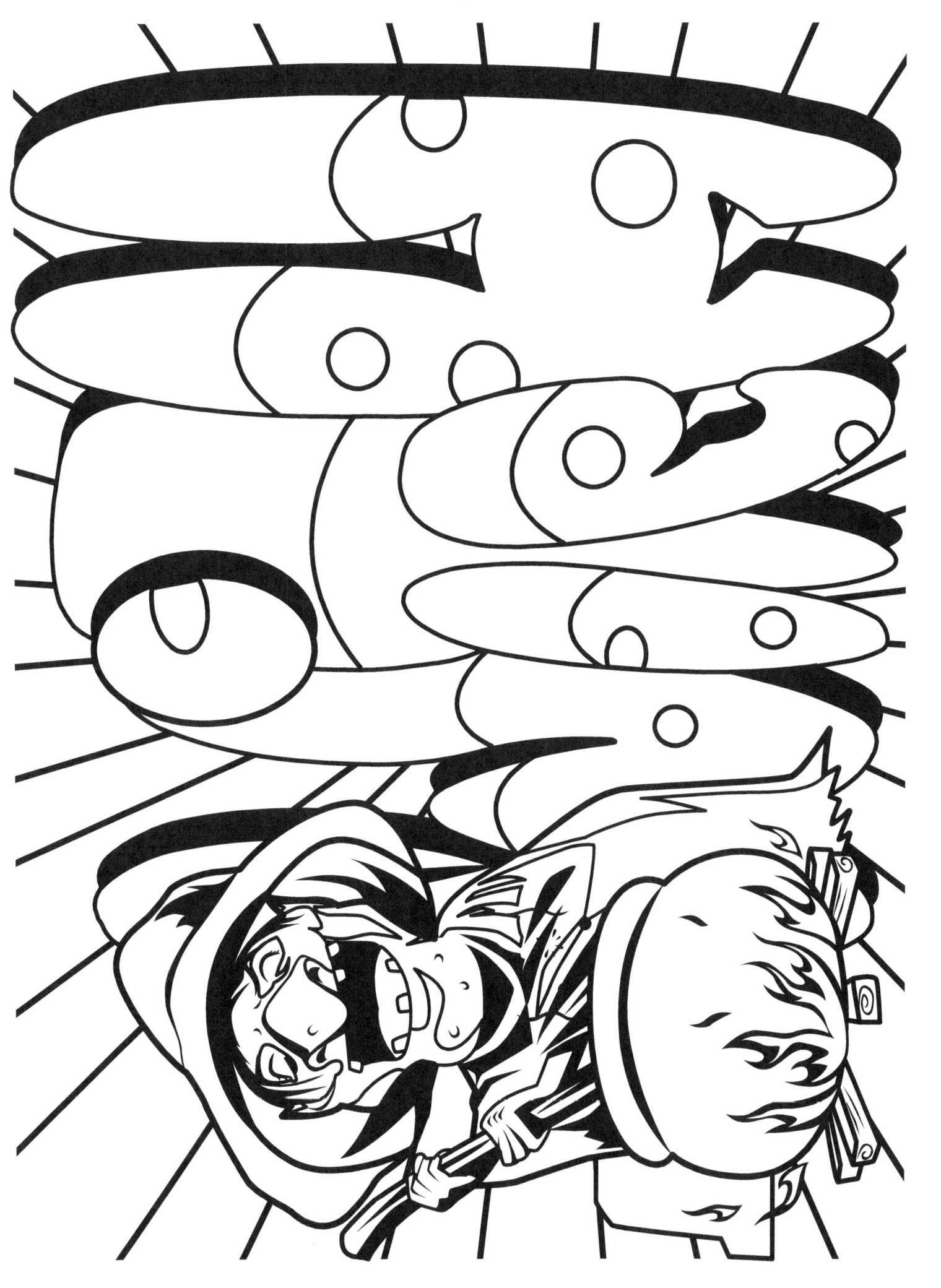

BLACK CAT

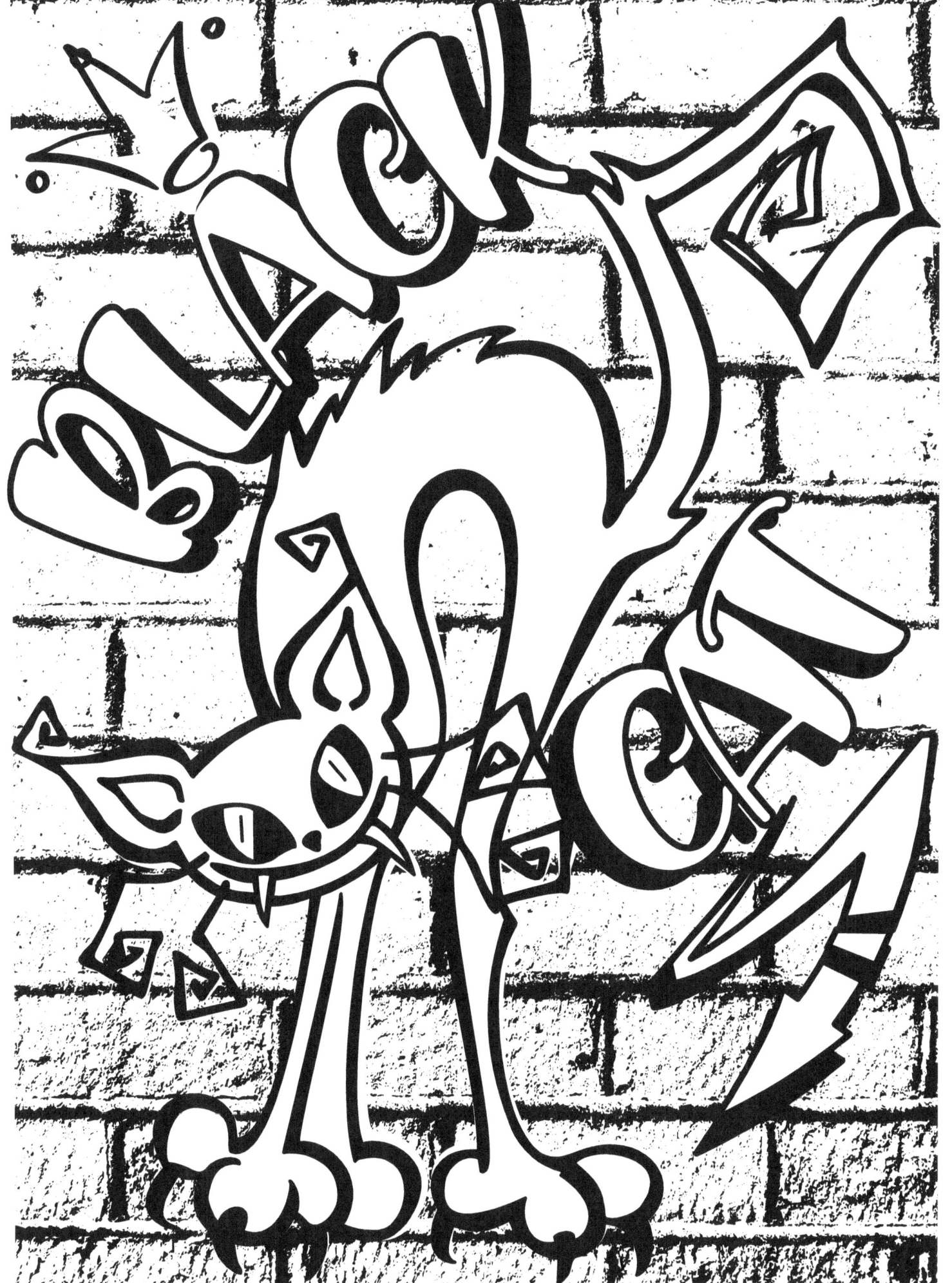

pumpkin

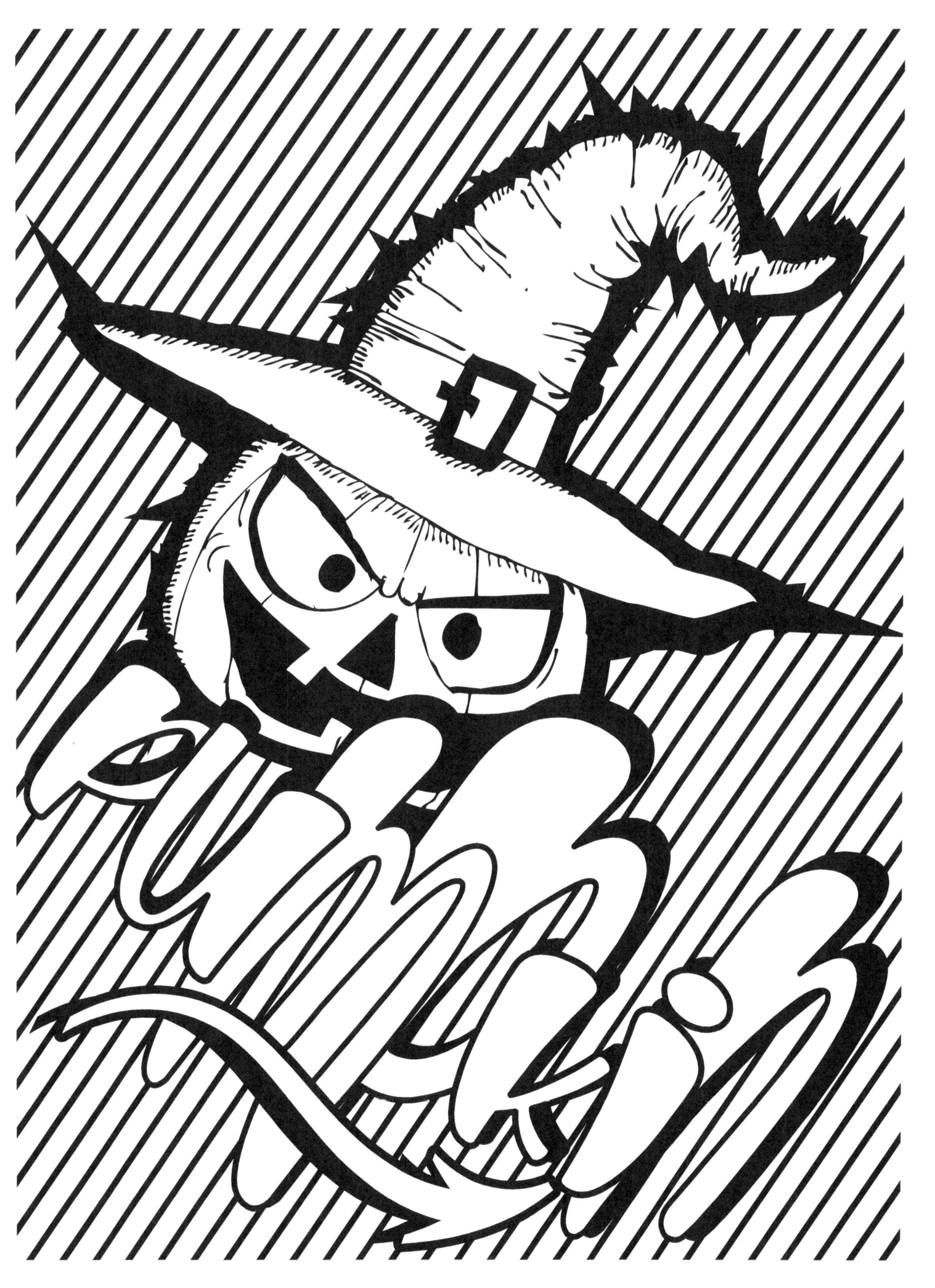

SCARECROW

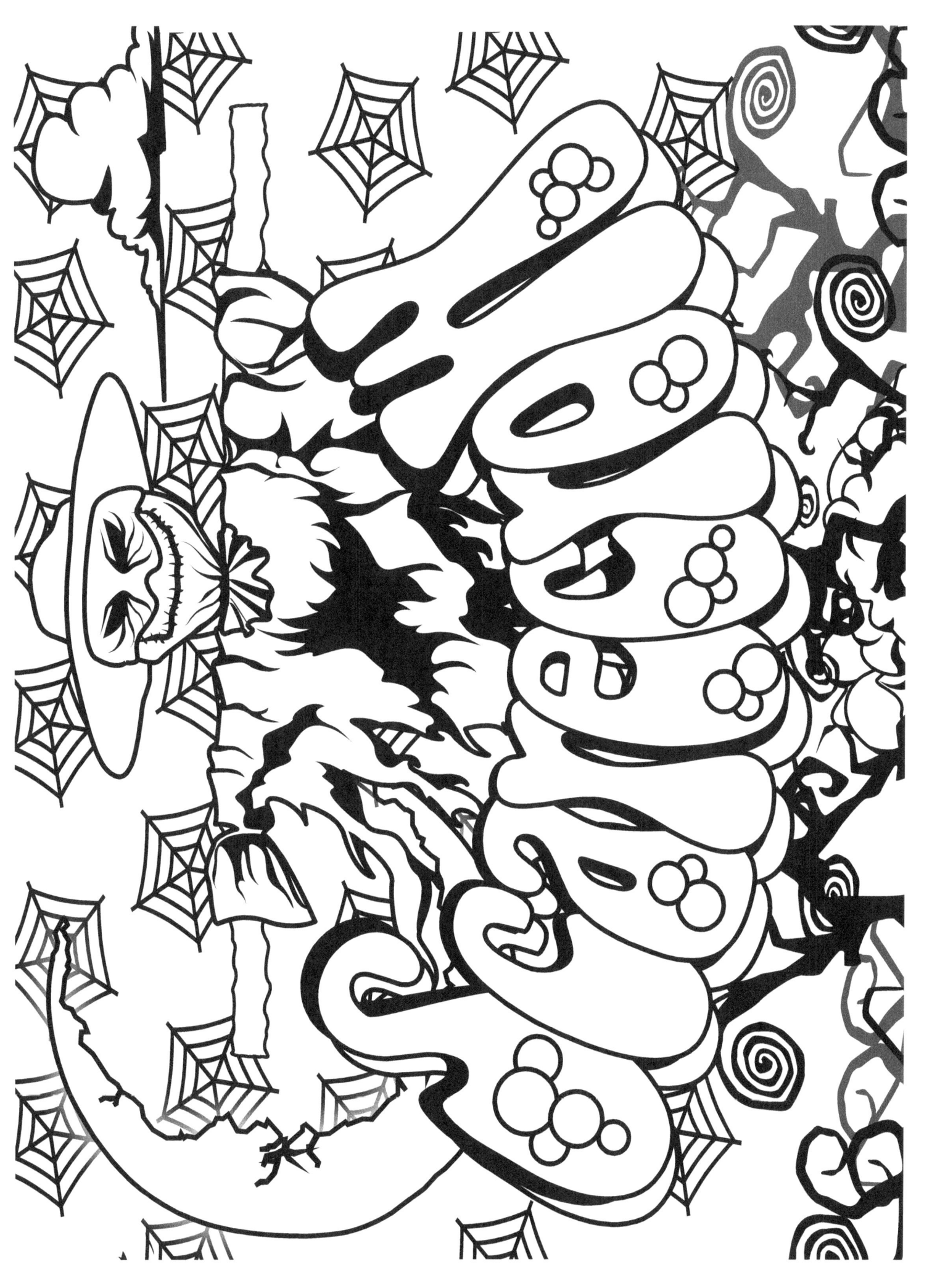

BOO

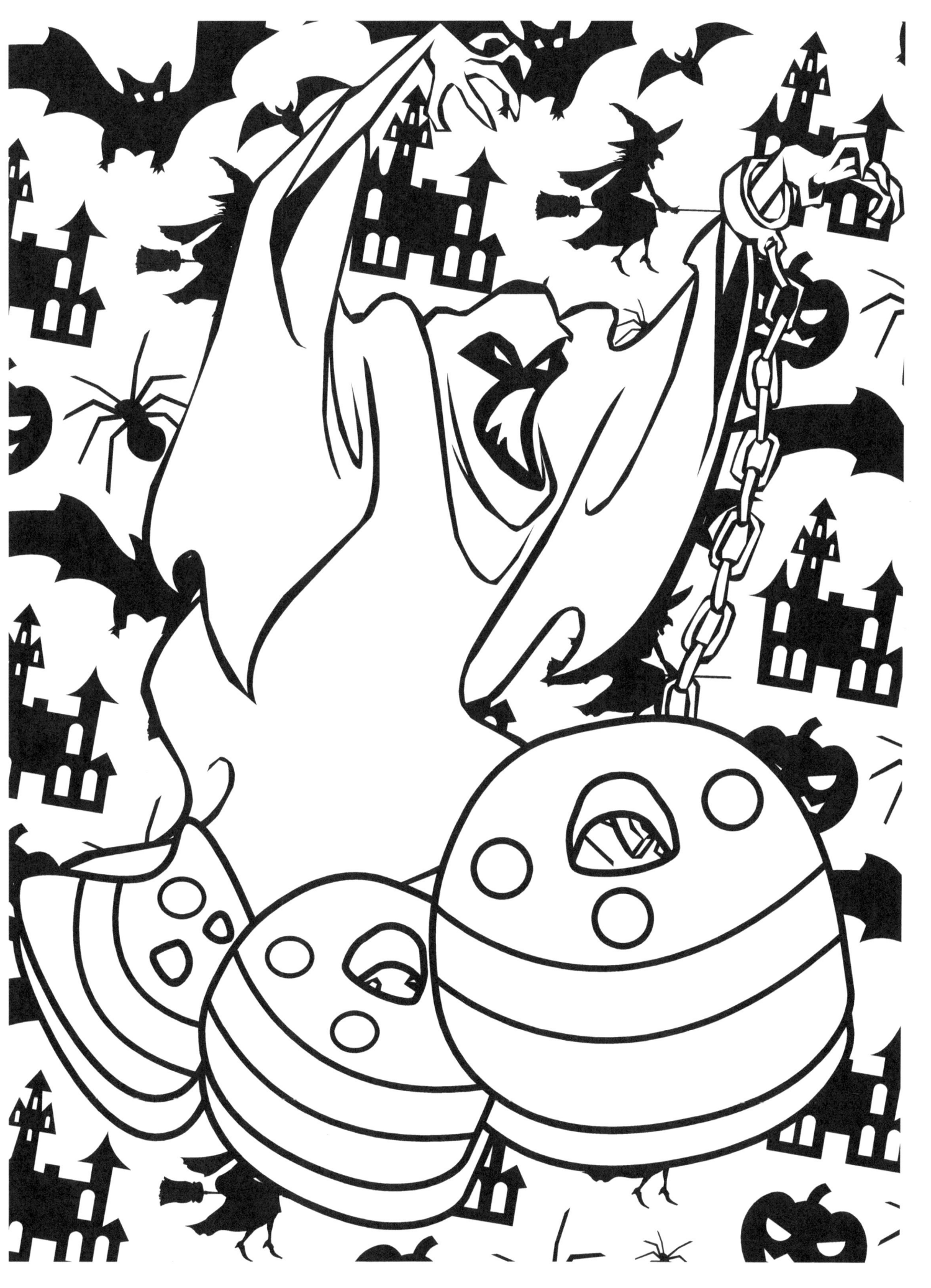

DRACULA

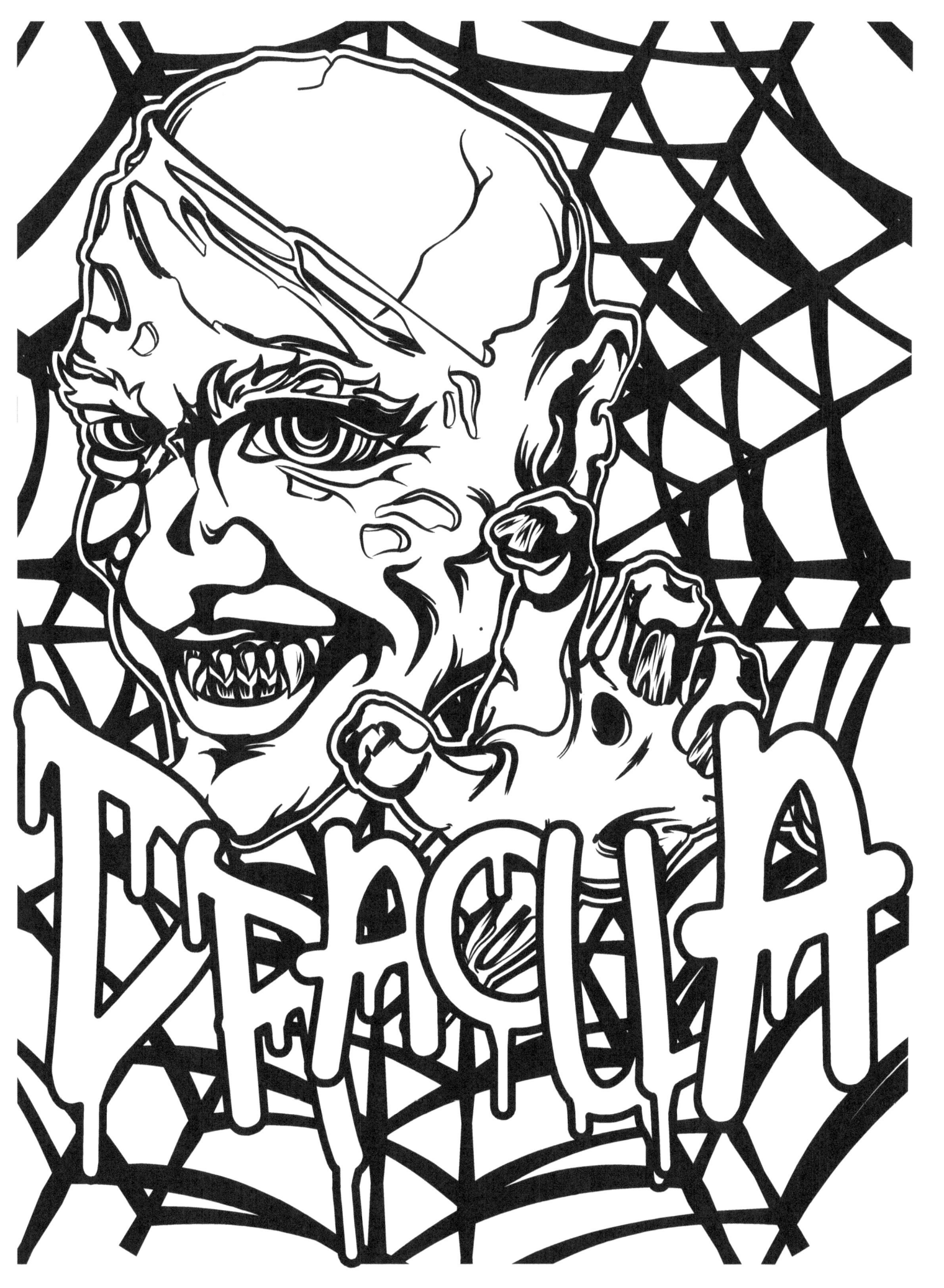

ZOMBIE KID

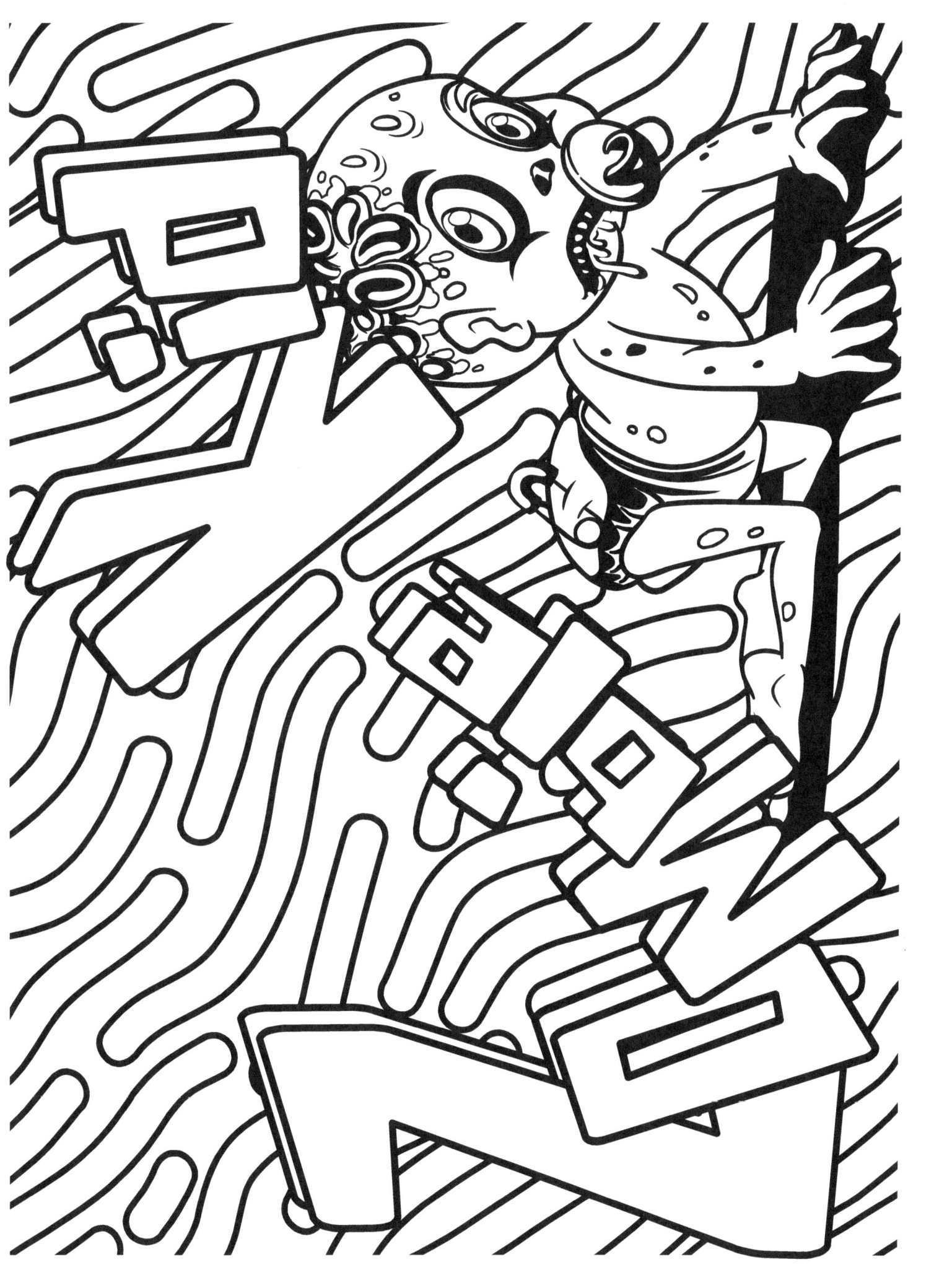

HALLOWEEN

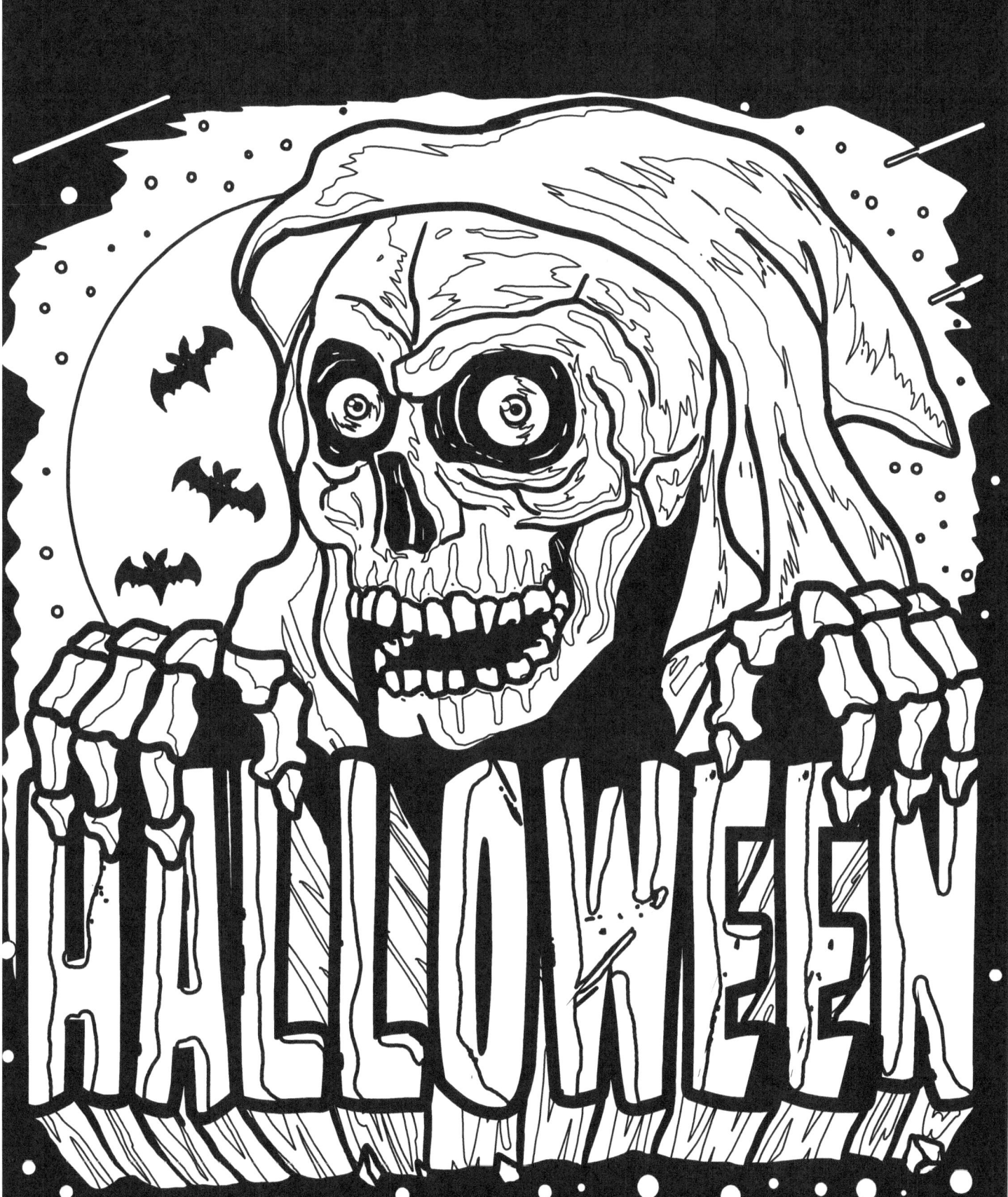

ZOMBIE DANCE

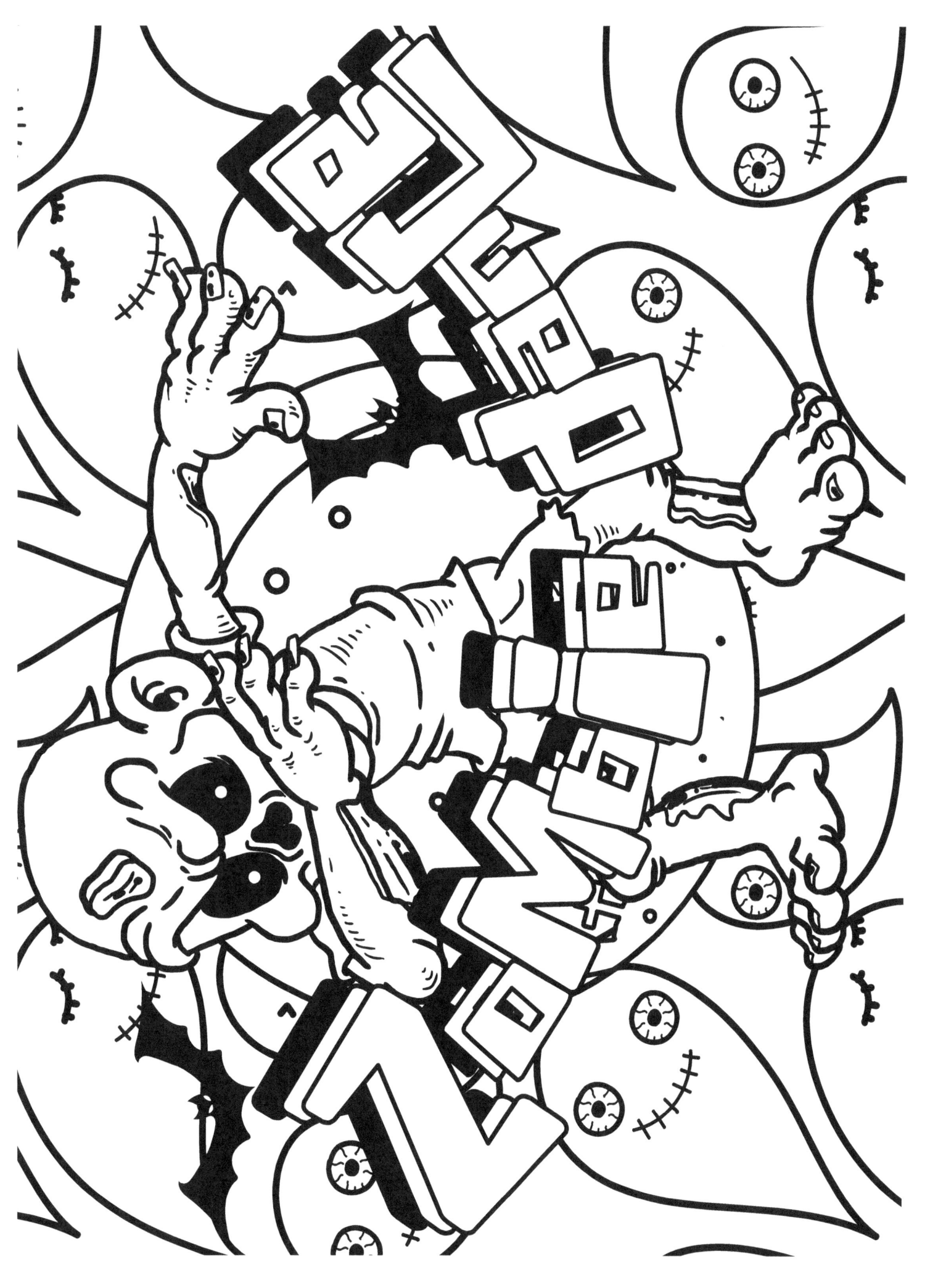

TRICK OR TREAT

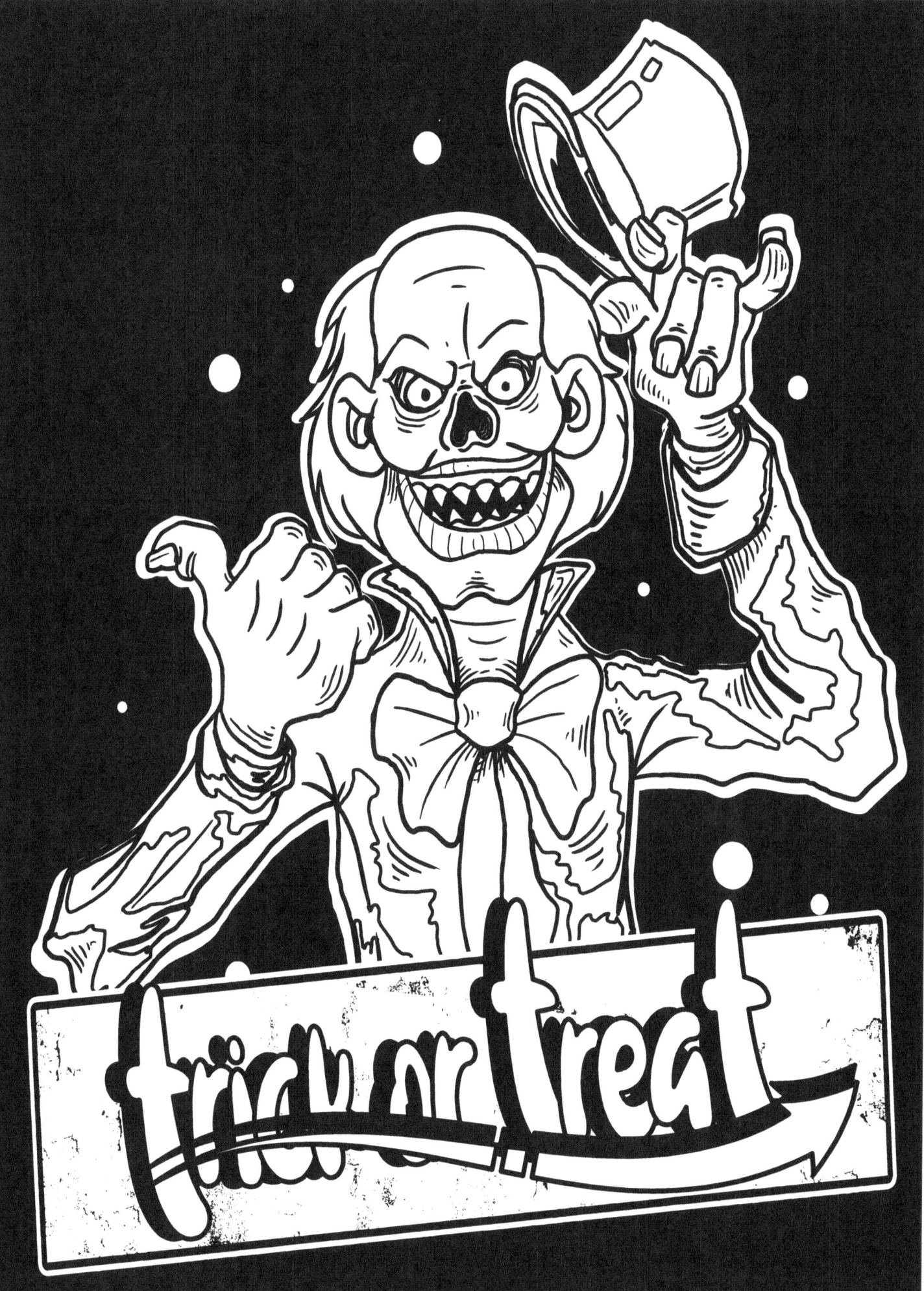

HALLOWEEN MUSIC

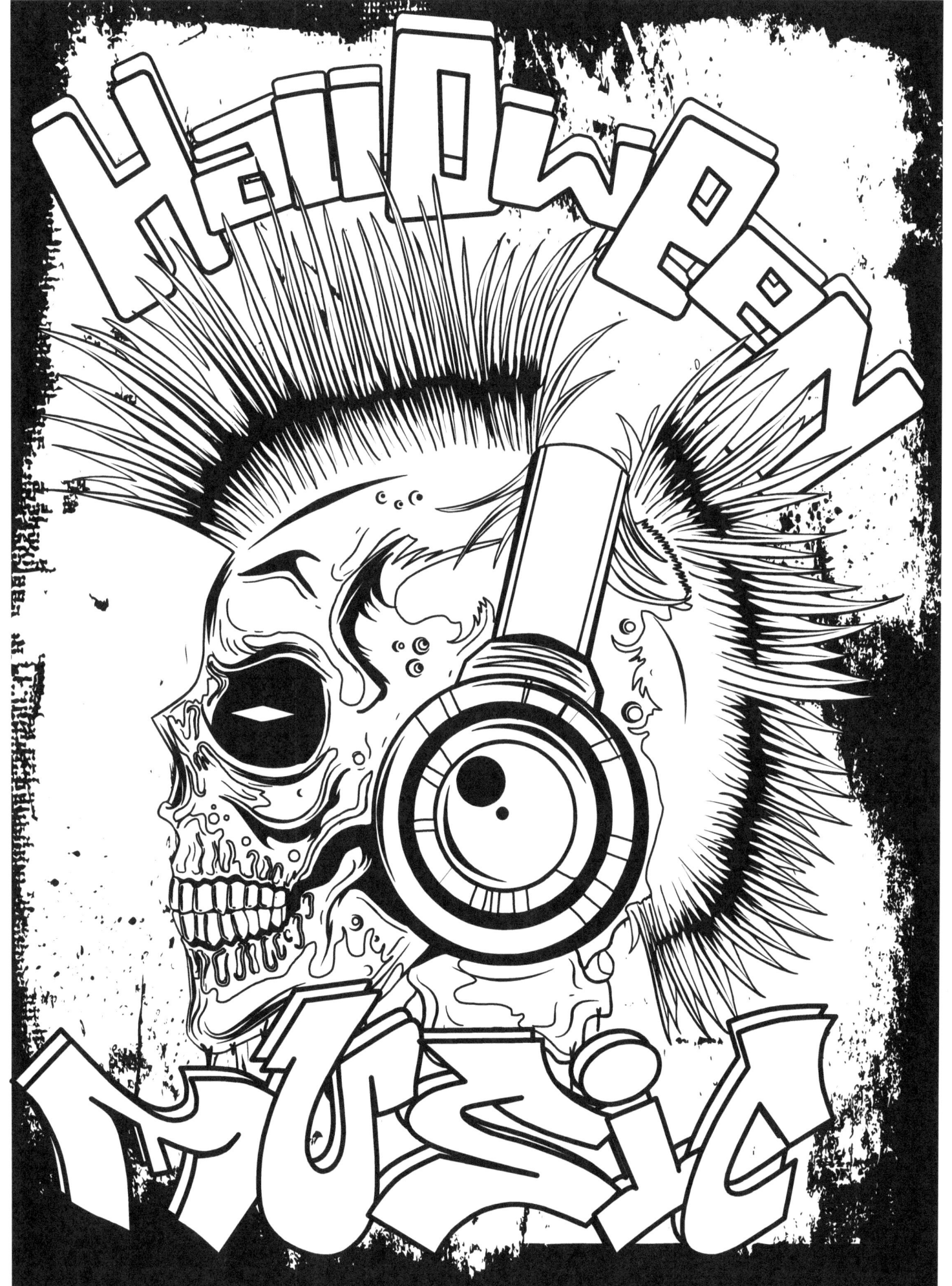

READY?

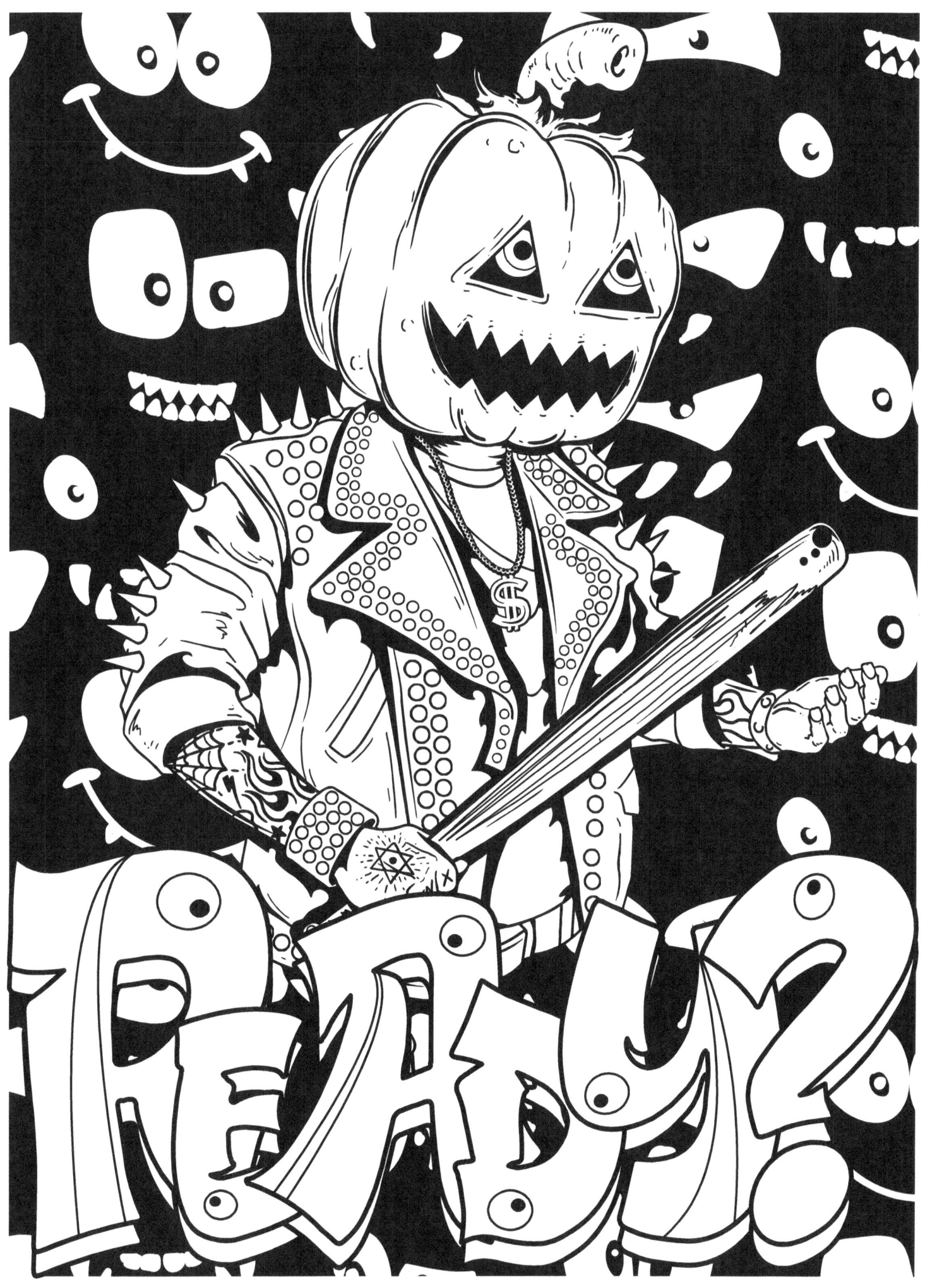

iT's Time!

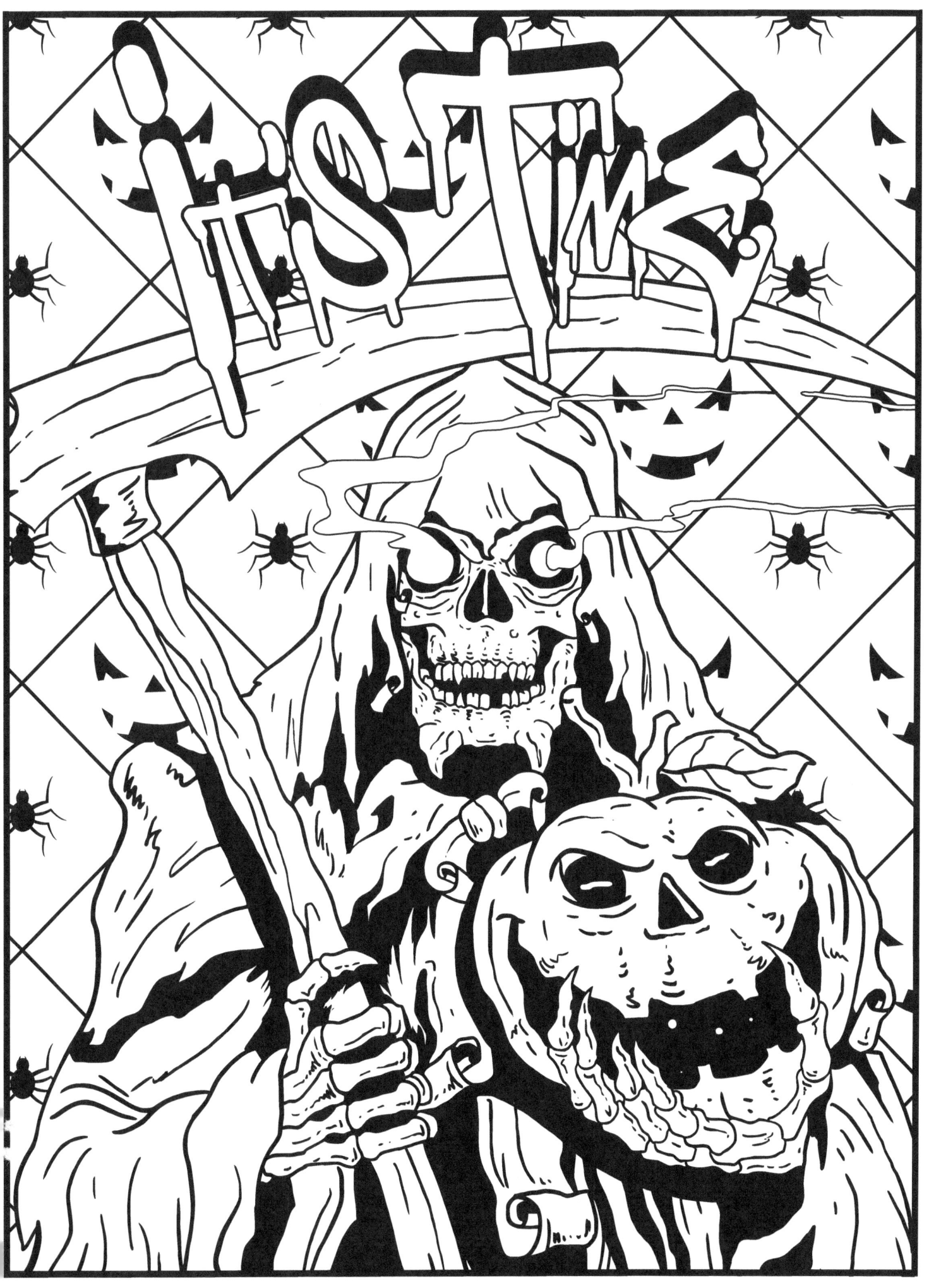

ZOMBIE NIGHT

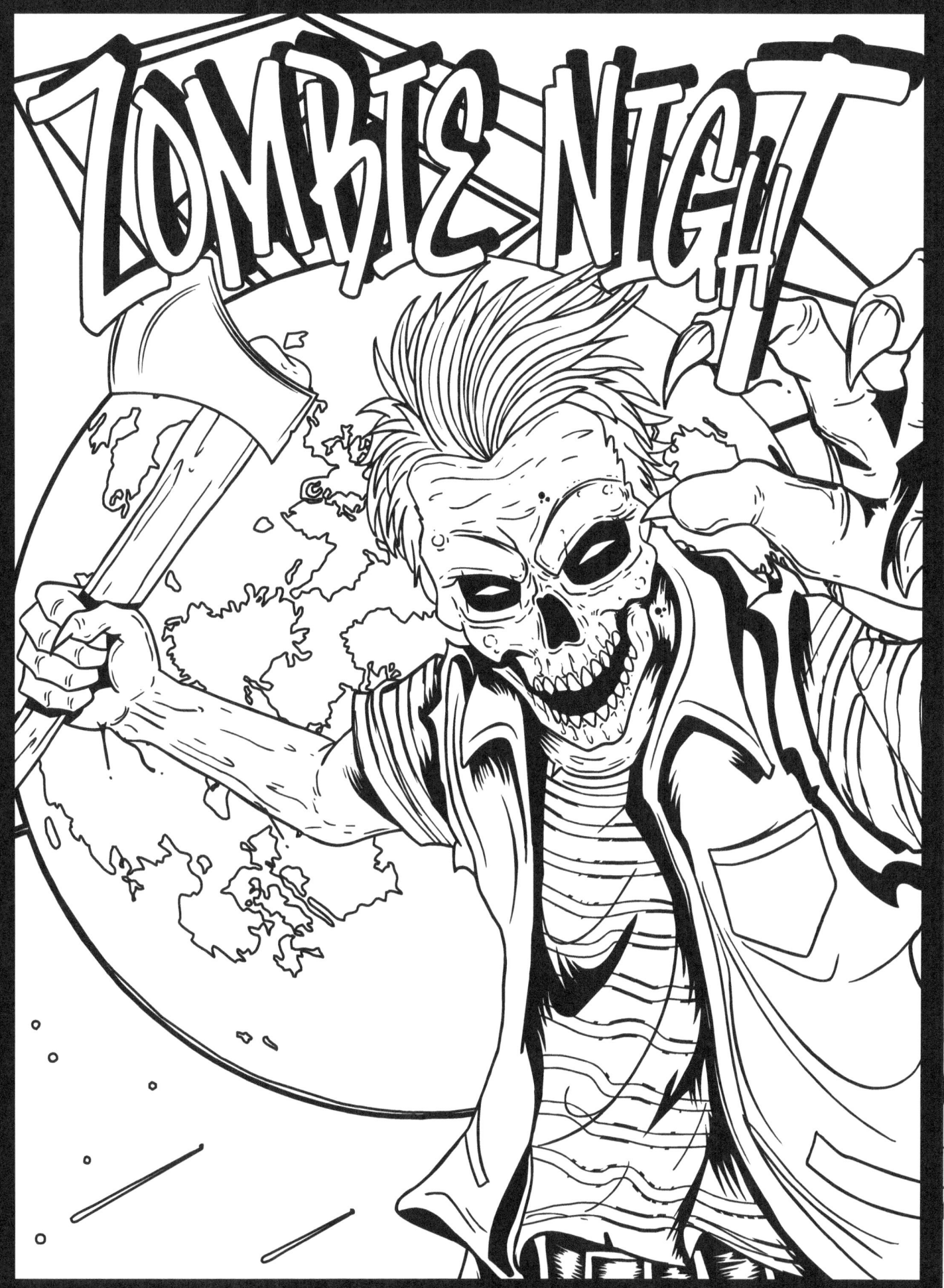

BATS

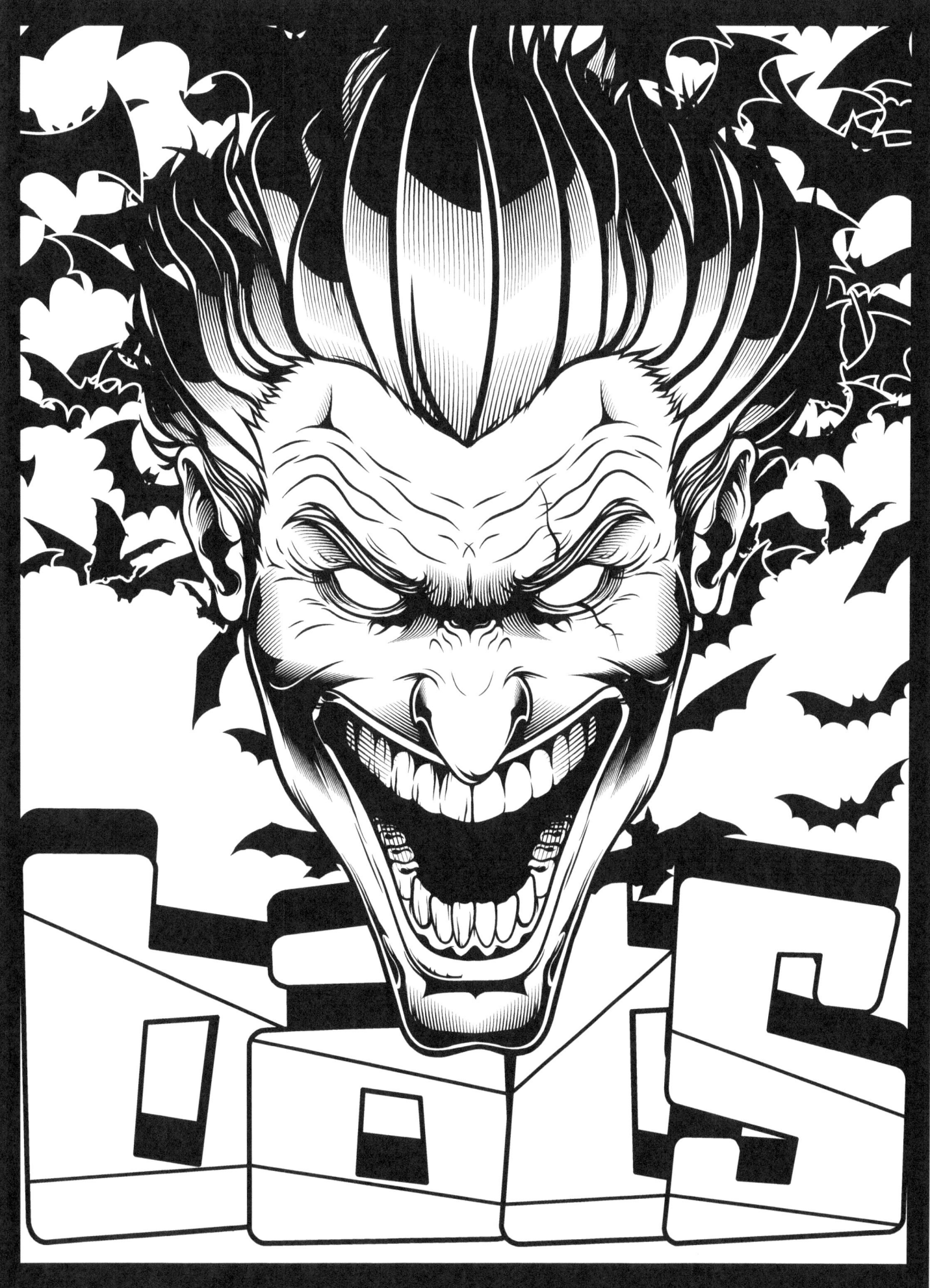

knock knock

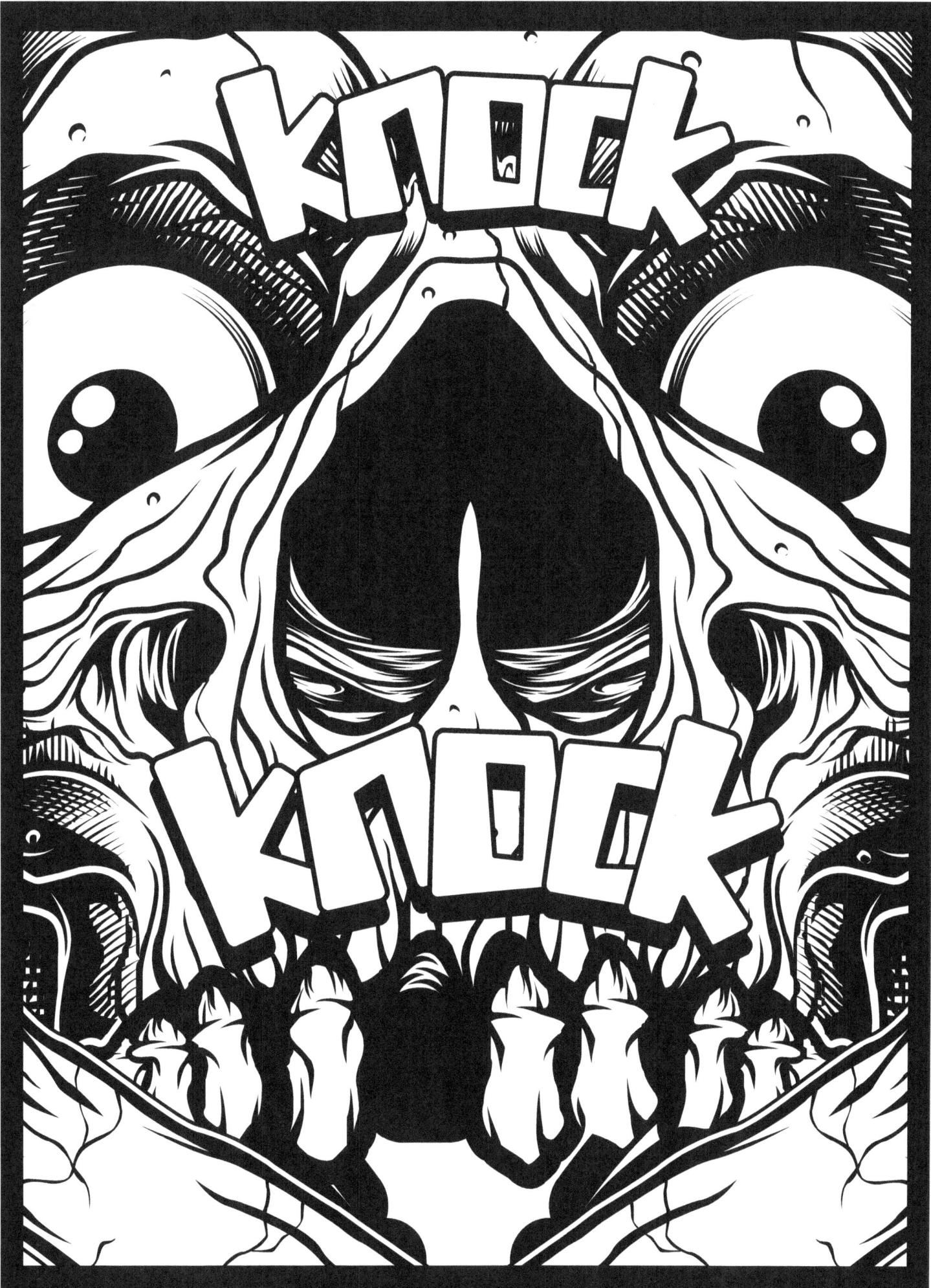

I see everything

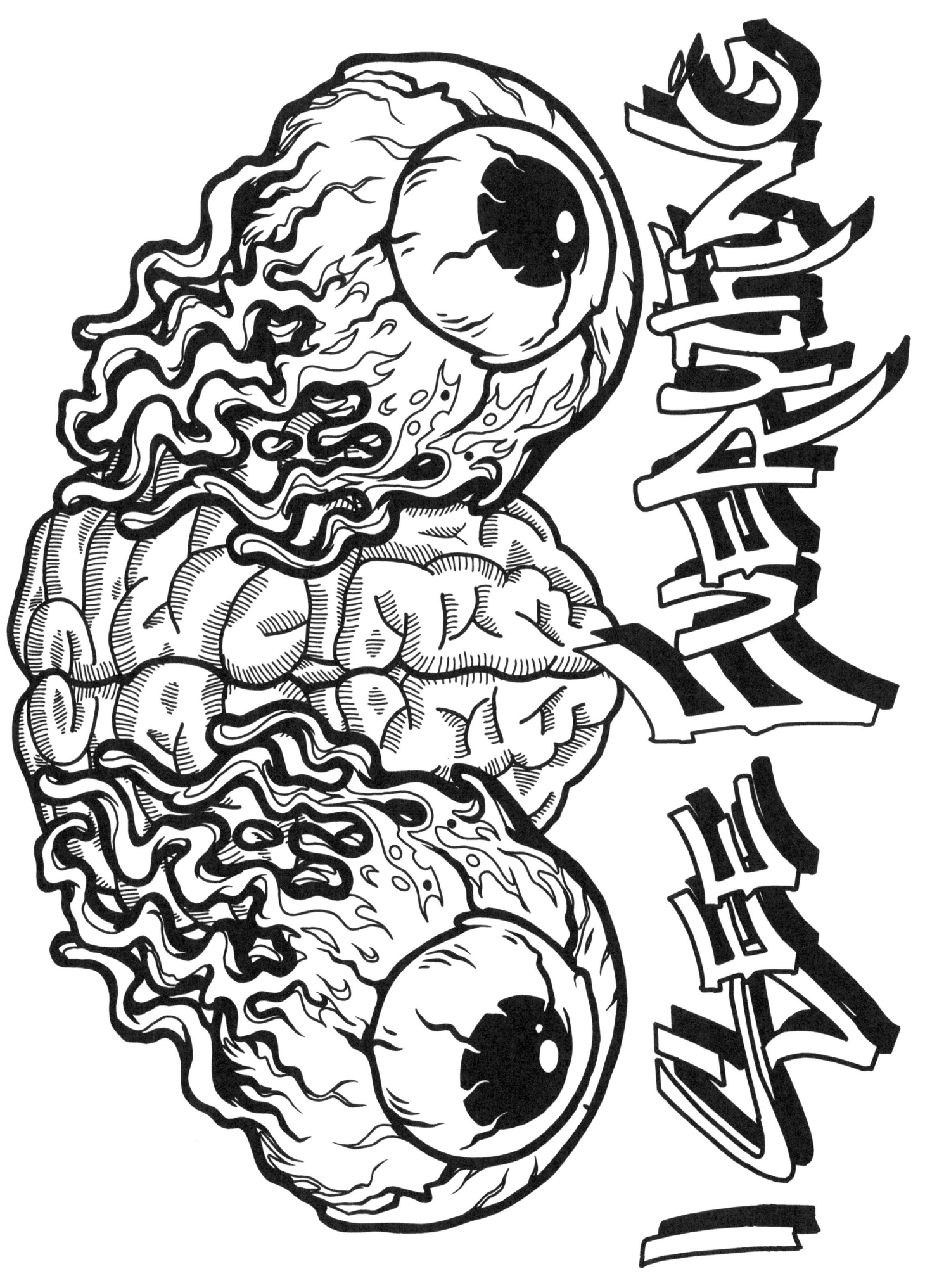

GRAVEYARD

MAGICAL NIGHT

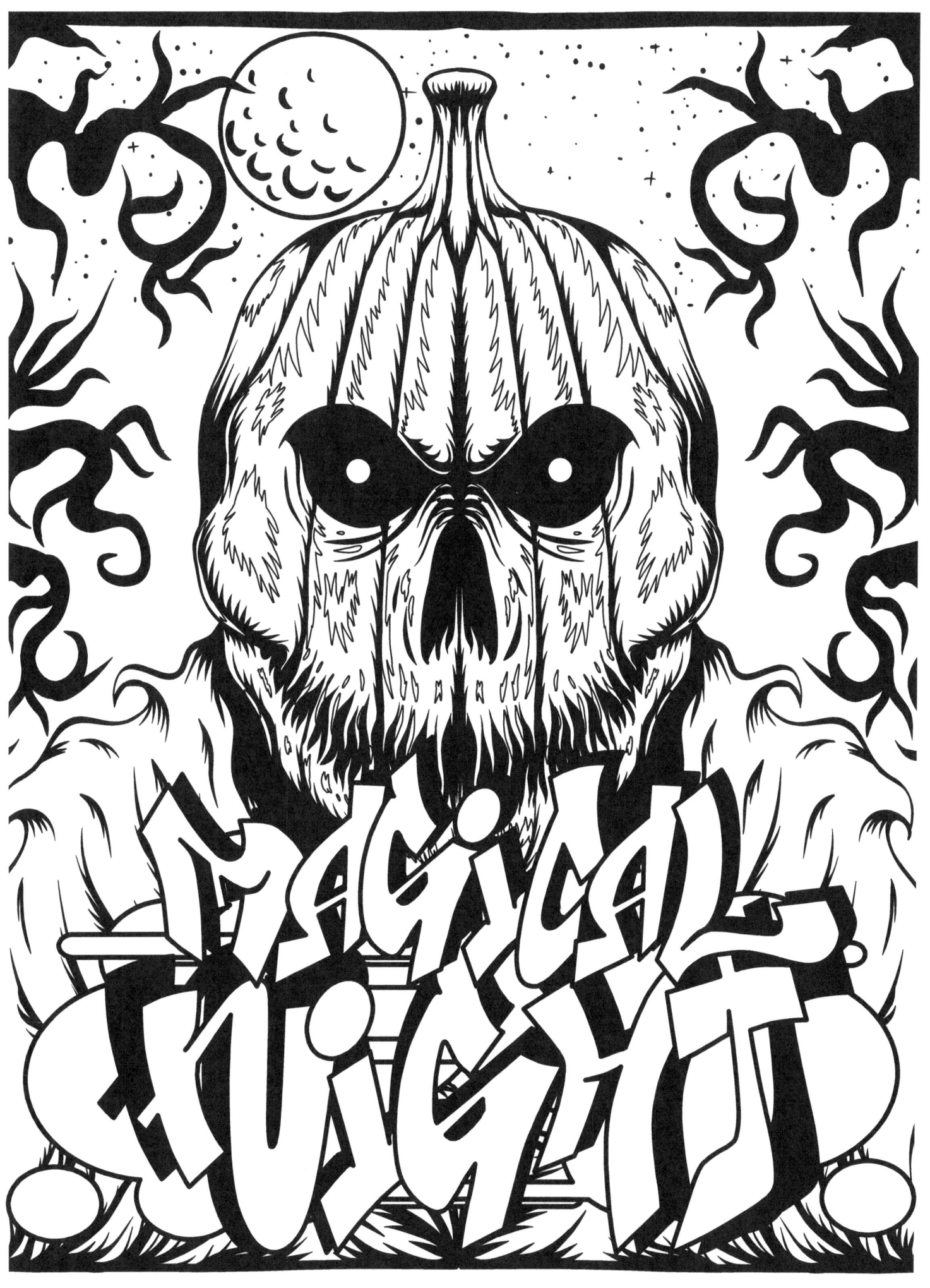

TRICK OR TREAT

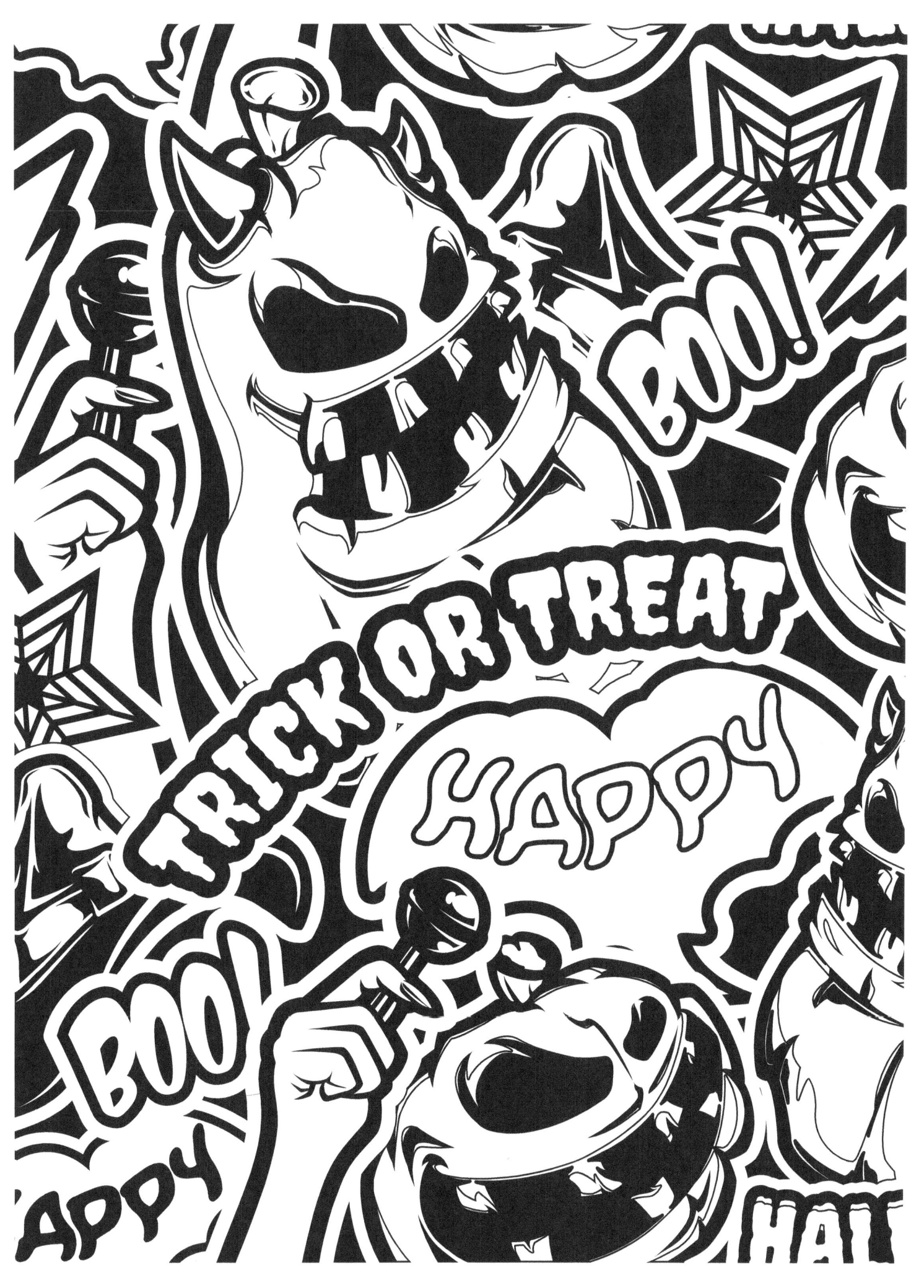

COOL

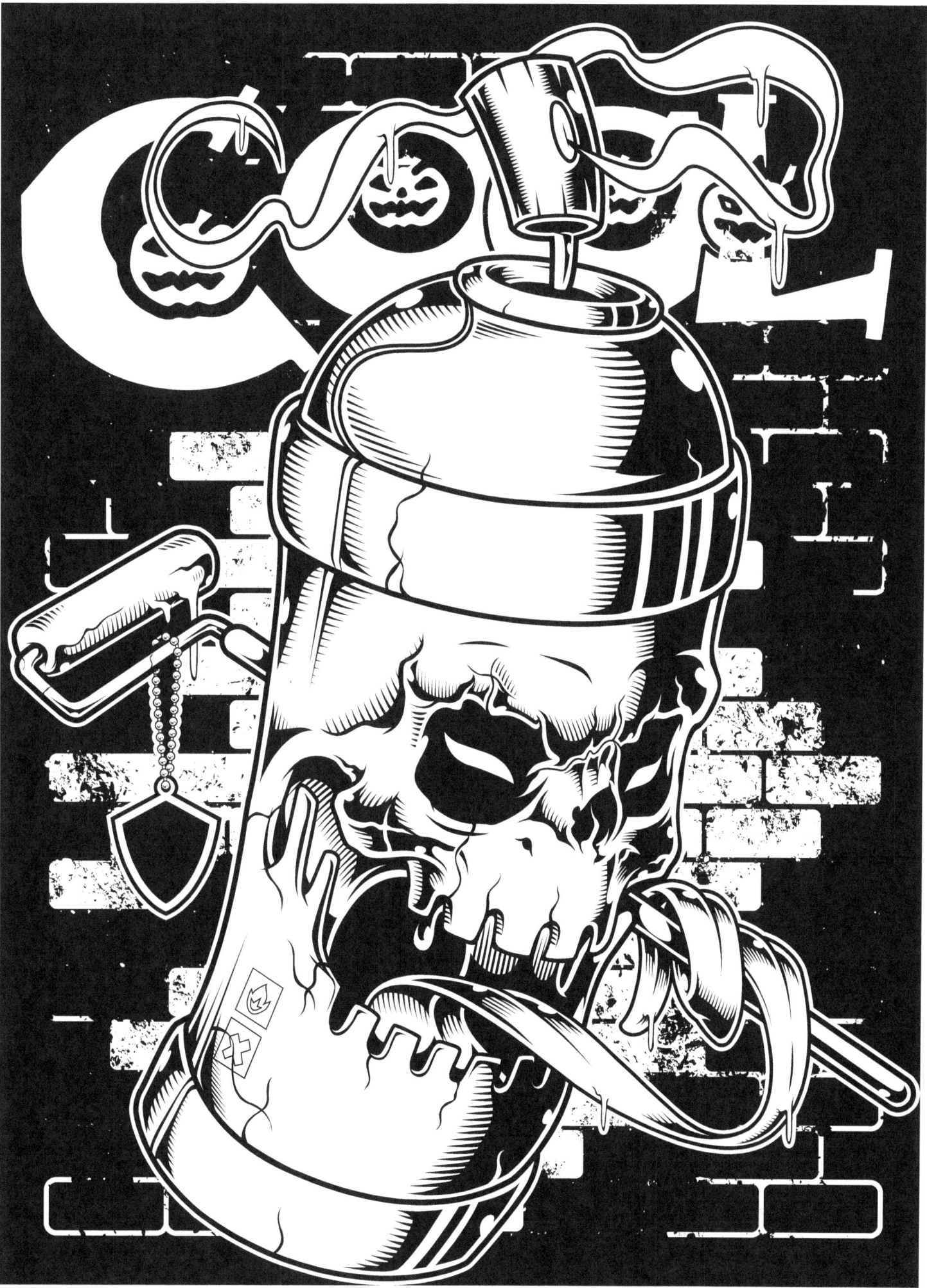

SPOOKY DRIVER

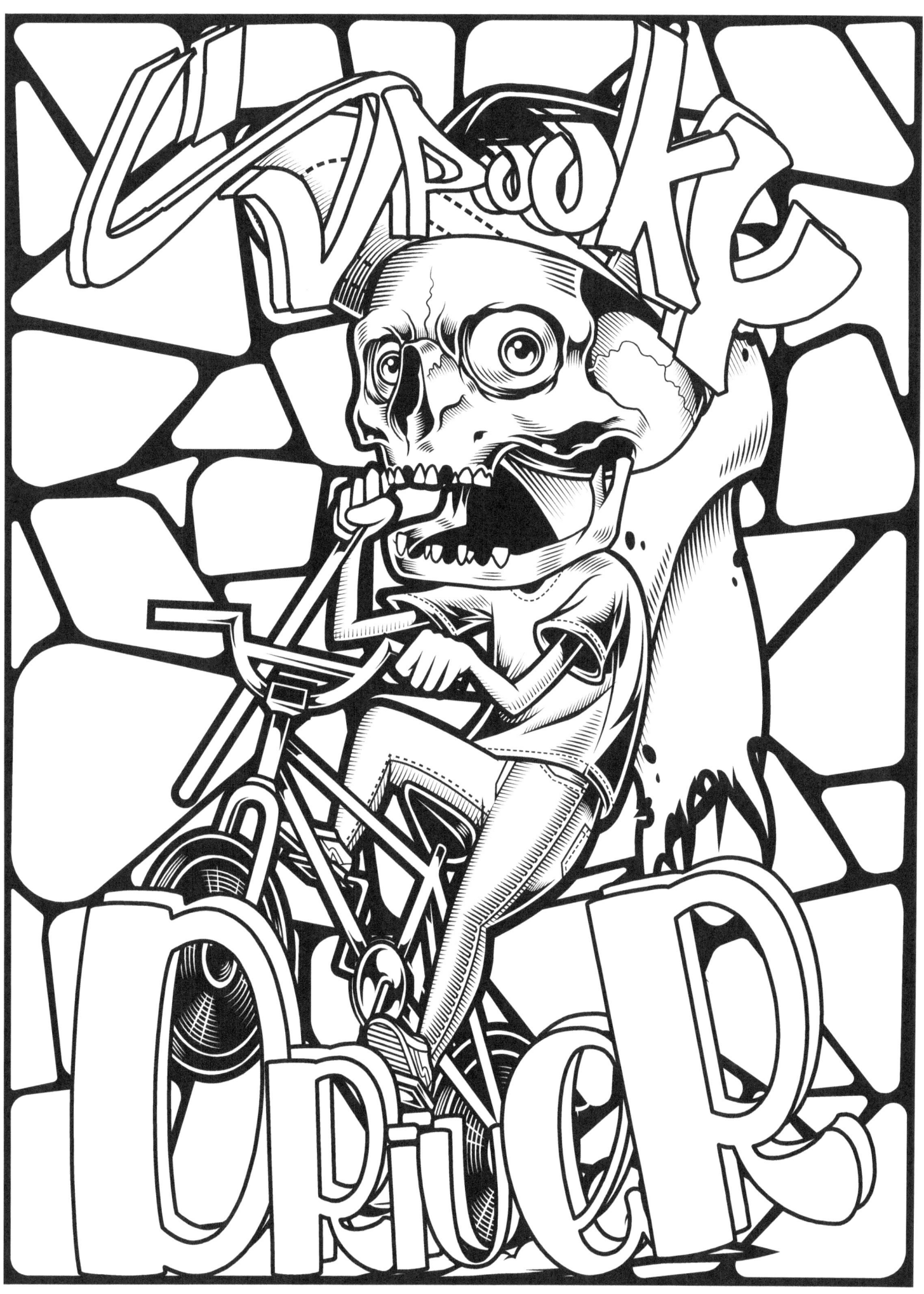

COFFee TiMe

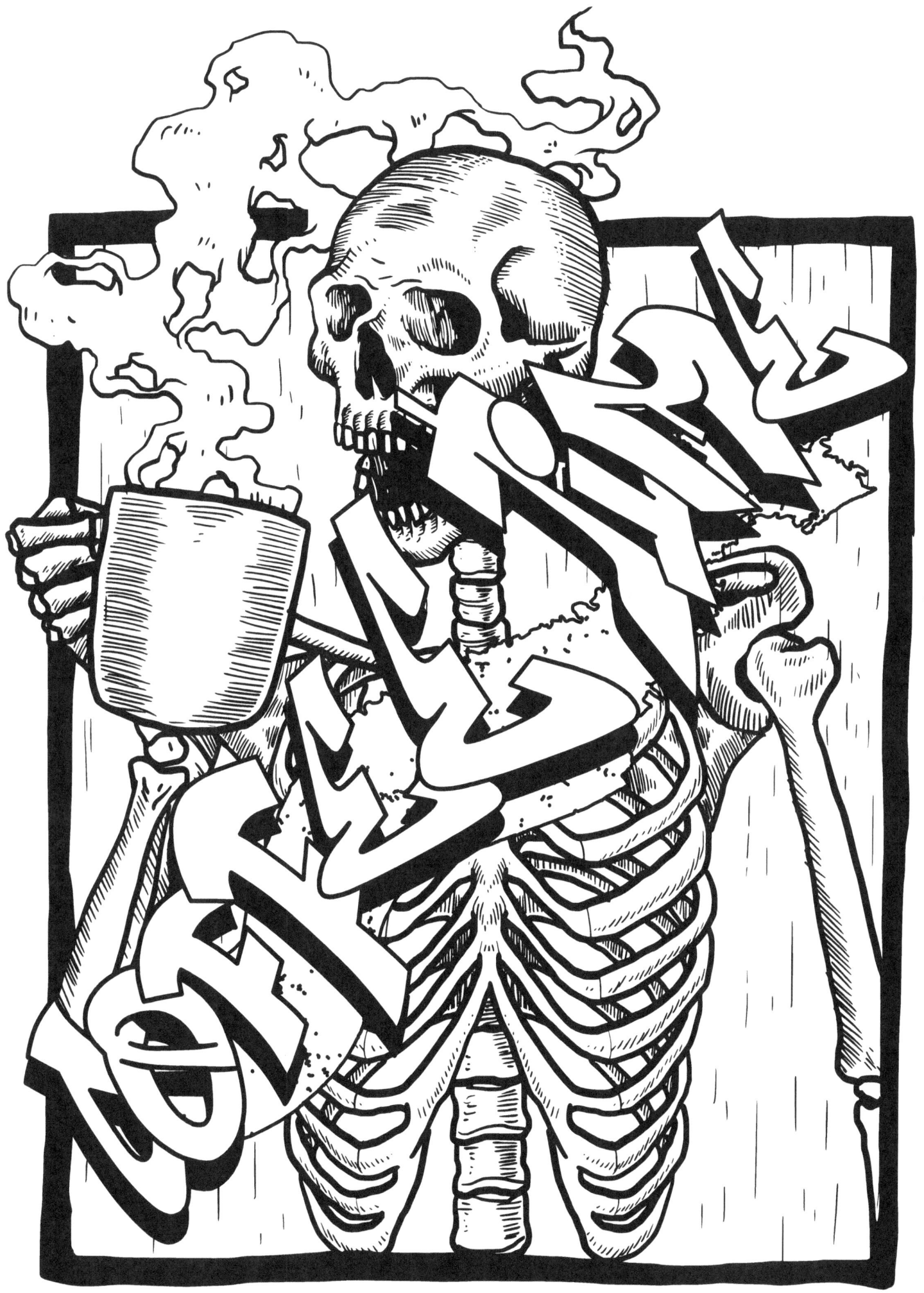

100% FUN

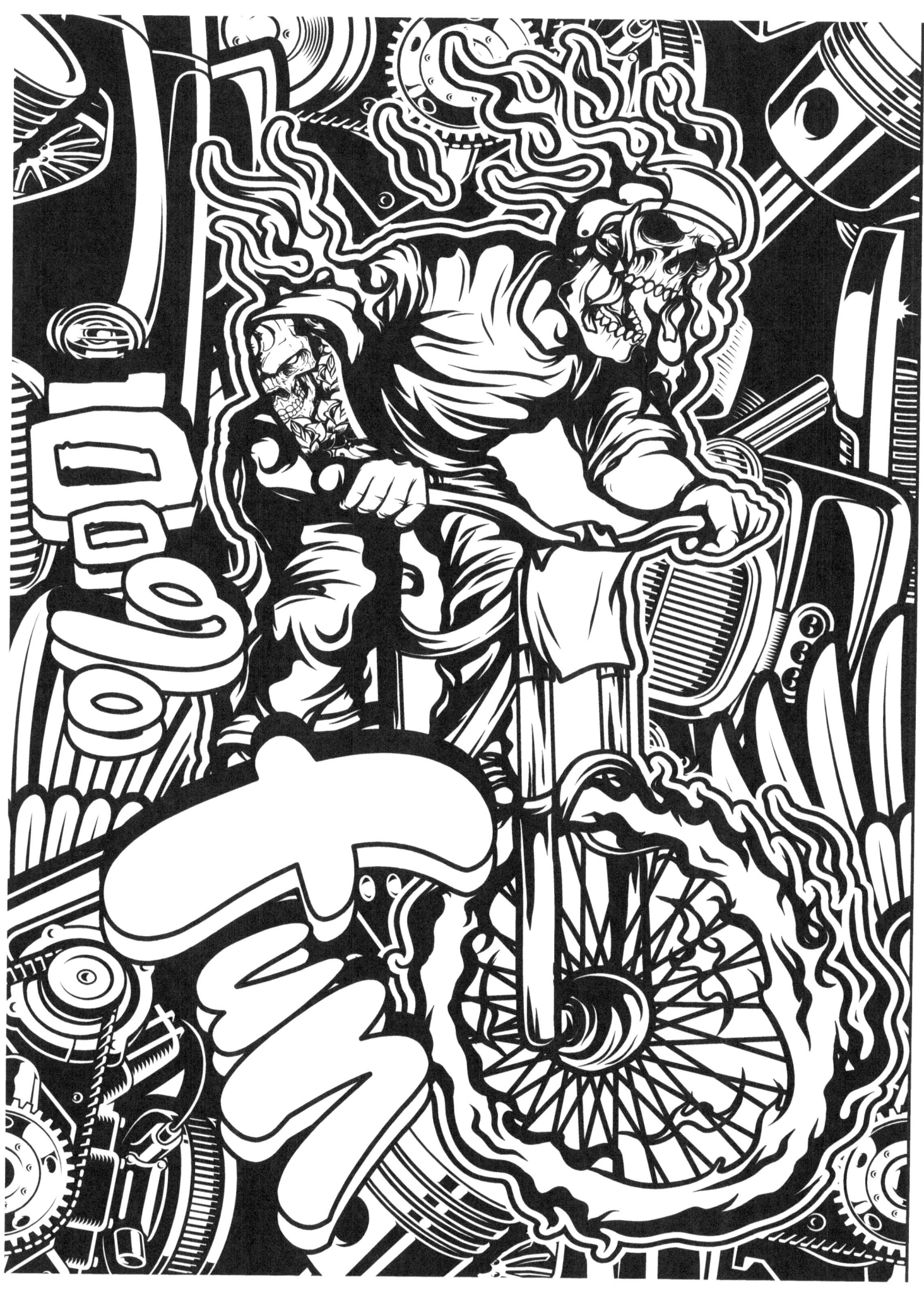

JUSTICE

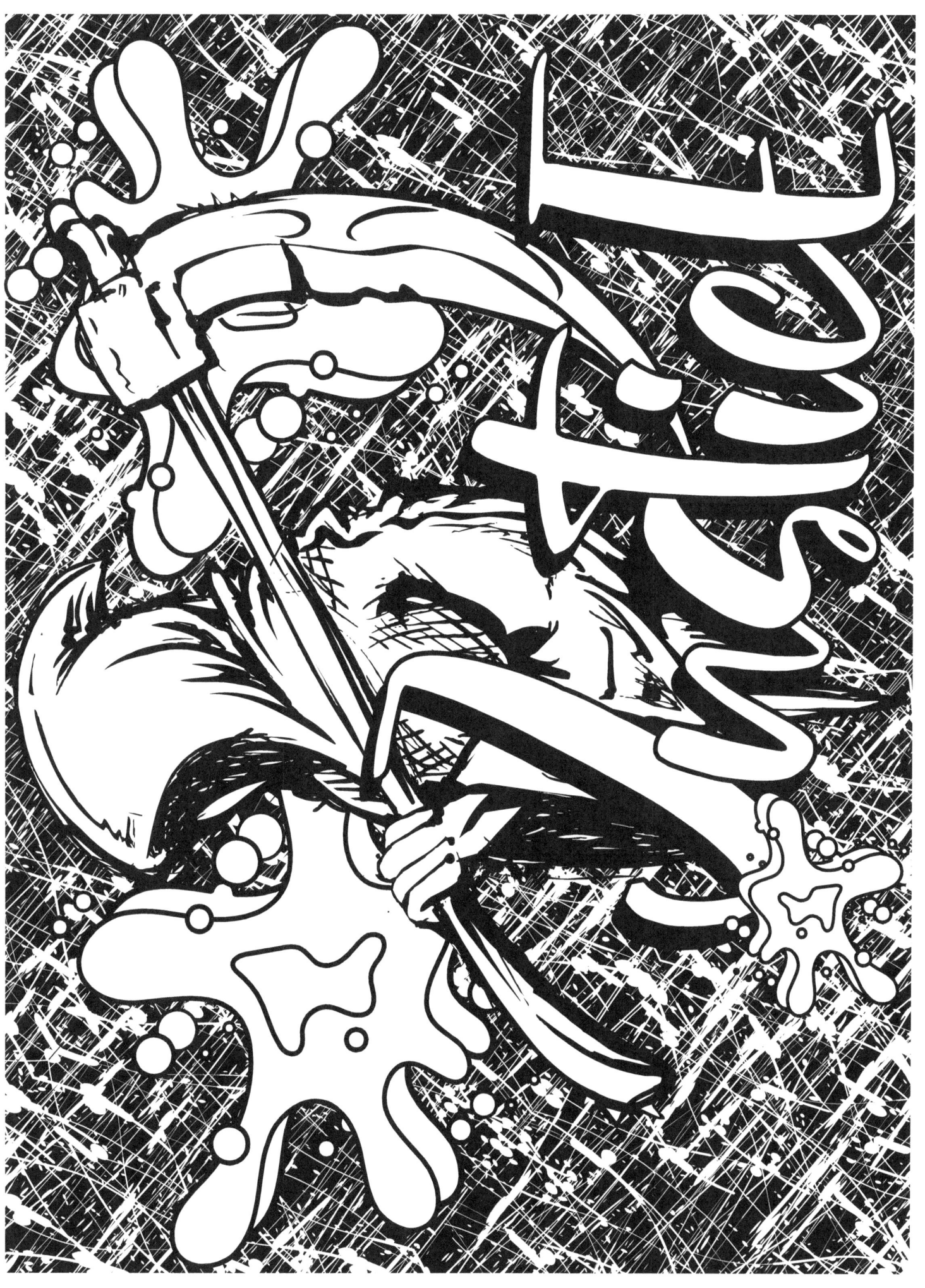

fire

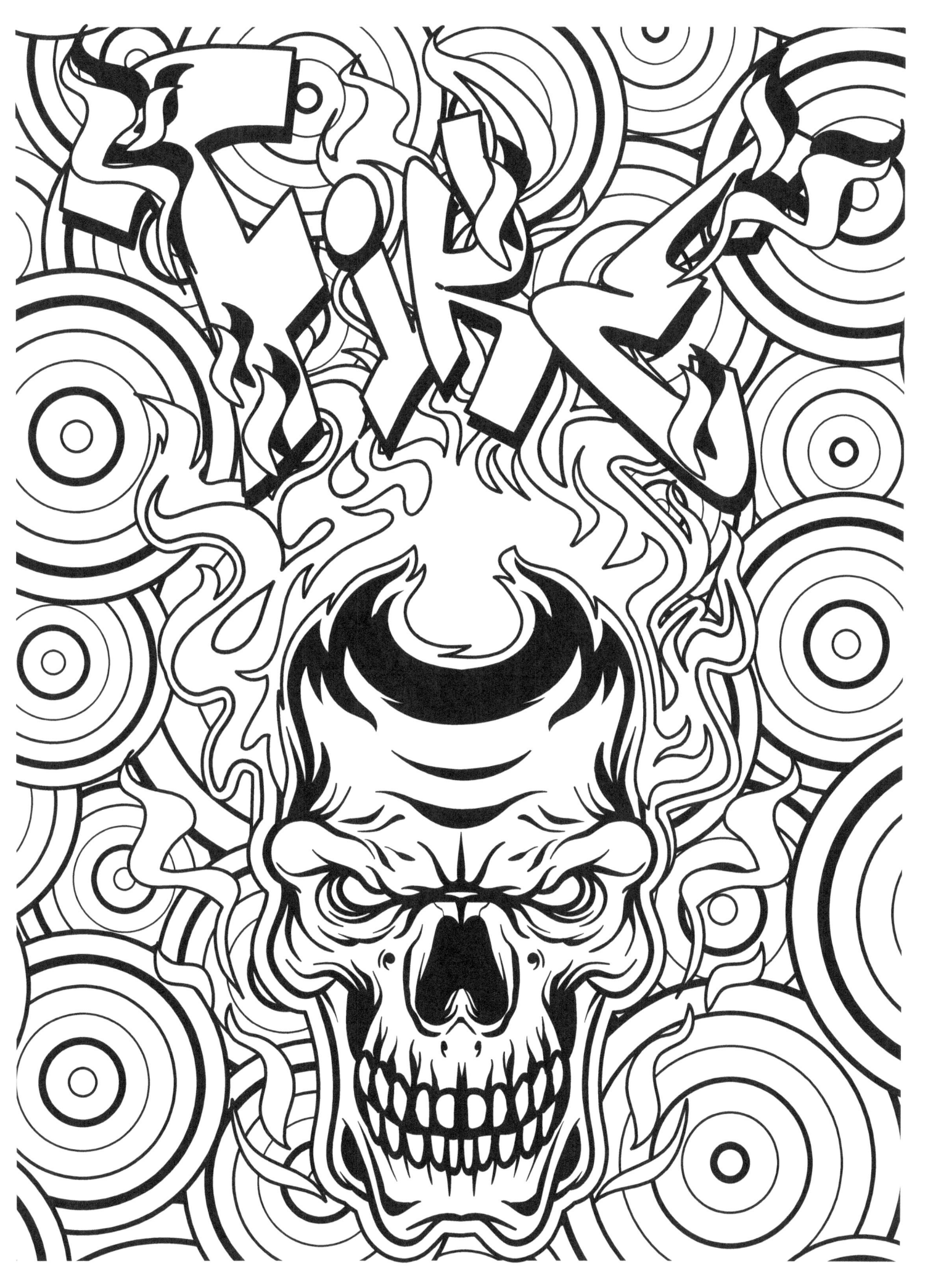

I'M SORRY

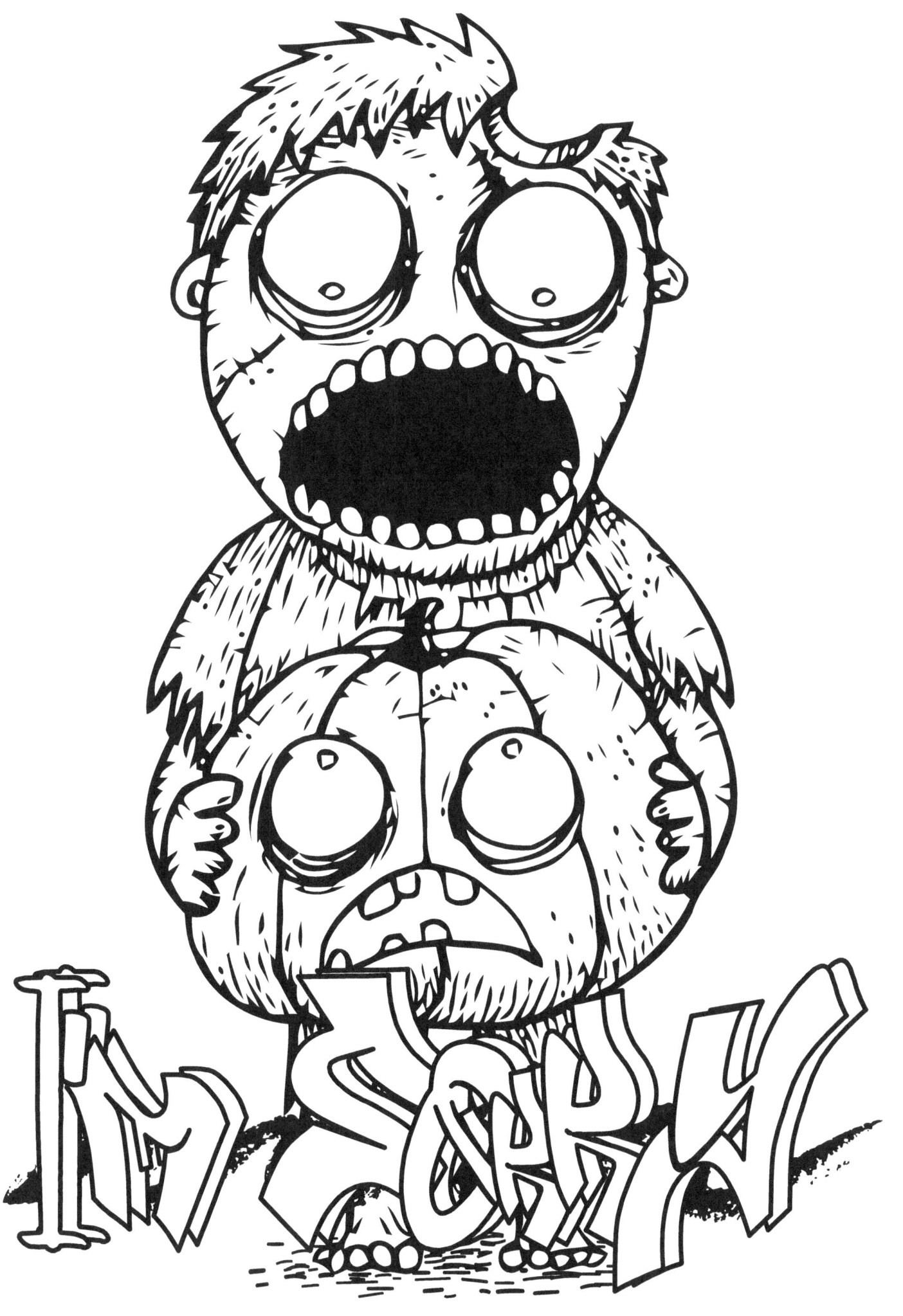

LET'S GO

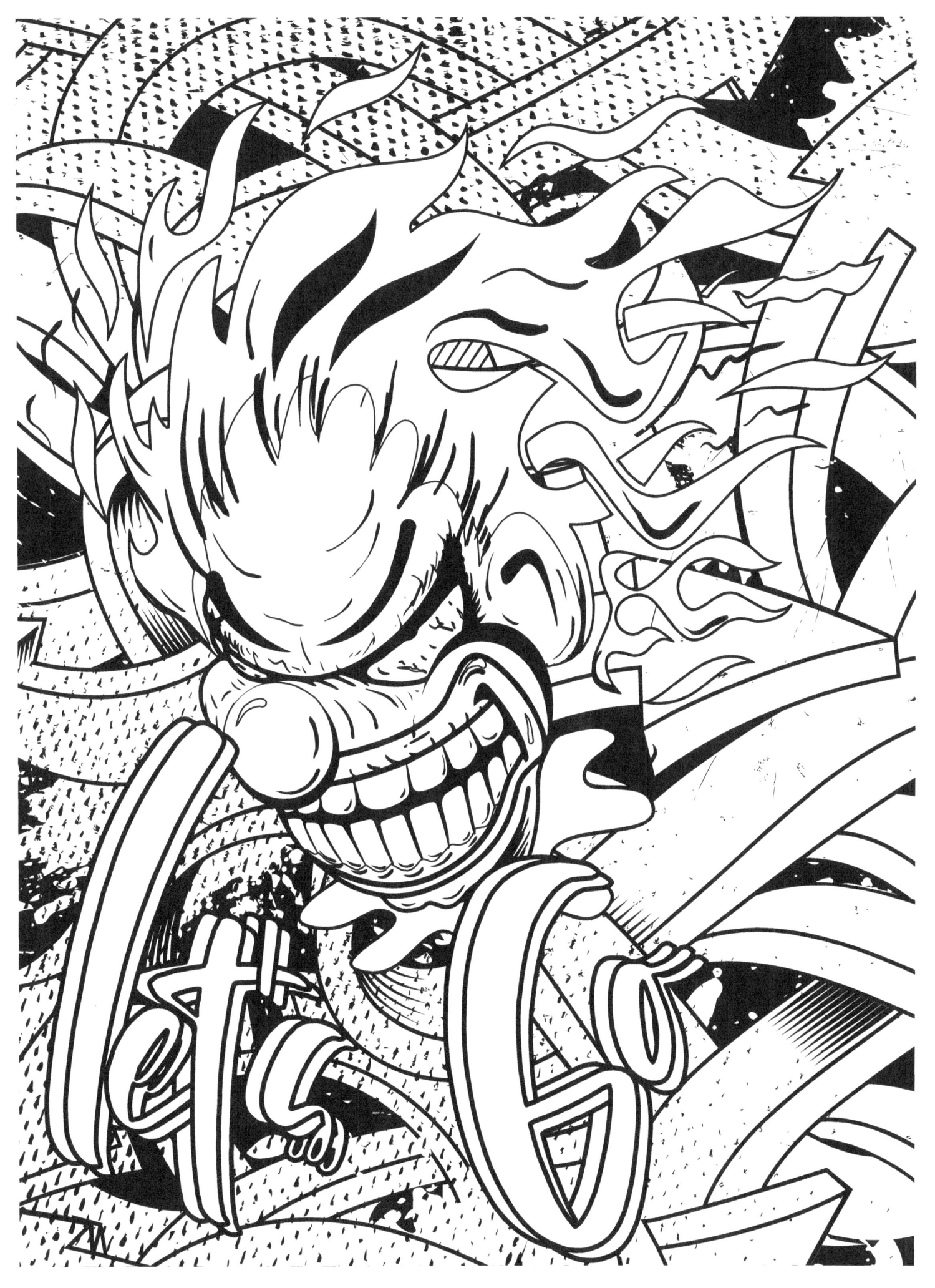